# Cancer, Sex, Drugs and Death

A Guide for the Psychological Management of Young People with Cancer

Dr Toni Lindsay

**AUSTRALIAN**ACADEMIC**PRESS**

First published 2017 by:
Australian Academic Press Group Pty. Ltd.
18 Victor Russell Drive
Samford Valley QLD 4520, Australia
www.australianacademicpress.com.au

Cancer, Sex, Drugs and Death: A Guide to the Psychological
Management of Young People with Cancer

ISBN    9781922117625 (paperback)
ISBN    9781922117632 (ebook)


Publisher: Stephen May
Copy editor: Tina Thornton
Cover design and typesetting: Luke Harris, Working Type Studio
Printing: Lightning Source

# Contents

# Acknowledgements

Firstly, and the most important acknowledgement needs to be for all of the young people and their families who I have worked with over the past 10 or so years. They have all been gracious in allowing me to walk next to them during some of the most difficult days of their lives. I have learnt something from each and every one of the young people and their families that I have met, and carry these lessons with me. These interactions are a daily reminder of what is important in our unpredictable world.

Secondly, there are people, who without their support, patience, friendship and guidance, I would not have developed the skills and knowledge to work in the way I do. So, Nicole Ferrar, Angela Cotroneo, Fran Orr, Rebecca Van Lloy, Emma Dickens, Catherine Adams, Julie Grove, Vivek Bhadri, Kristyn Schilling, Joan Ryan and Clayton Barr thank you for all of your time, expertise and practice wisdom. A special mention to Cath and Julie who have opened my eyes to the tiny details that make you both incredible therapists, it's an honour that you share your thoughts with me.

Eileen, Catherine and Michael – your individual support over the past years, as well as all of the support from Chris O'Brien Lifehouse broadly has kept myself, and all of the psycho-oncology team on track. The Adolescent and Young Adult service has flourished over the past years by the hard work of many dedicated people, and we can see the benefit to our young patients every day, but most especially on the days when it feels the toughest. To both the Psycho-Oncology and Allied Health teams at Lifehouse, you all work above and beyond, it doesn't go unnoticed.

To Stephen at Australian Academic Press, thanks for taking on this project, and for all the support as I bumbled through my first book. Thanks to the editing team who made sense of the first drafts.

I would also like a huge mention to all of the people in my world who provide all of the important life stuff. Friendships that have spanned over years, as well as incredible family; Gayleen, Ian, Renee, Charlotte, Sue, Ange, Bec, Nik, Sarah and Shelley. I don't have an adequate way of saying thank you, other than Thank you!!!!

And, T. You give the support, lots of ideas and instil a sense that all of this can be done. We are a good team.

# Preface

The purpose of this book is not to teach readers how to be clinicians. Instead, it is about upskilling clinicians who are already working therapeutically to extend into the oncology (and other healthcare settings) with young people and their families. The writing and case studies included form the basis of exploring the clinical implications of treatment, diagnosis, survivorship and end of life, and the way that young people experience and negotiate through these things. Cancer makes life complex and more challenging, both while treatment is happening and when it is completed, and by being able to identify the normal reactions that young people experience, therapeutic interventions and management of psychological symptoms is much easier.

This book is not based on research exclusively, rather it has a very strong clinical focus. This does not mean that research is not important, of course, it forms the underpinning of what is done in the clinical setting. However, I have personally always found learning via other people's clinical experience more rich and valuable, which is my goal for this book. The case studies and examples, as well as clinical guides, are a culmination of many years of experience working with young people and their families. All the case studies are a combination of many young people, rather than an individual, but they are the stories that some are unable to tell for themselves.

The way that I envisage this book being most helpful is for it to provide guidance and structure when working with young people in an environment that can be unpredictable and uncertain. I would like the book to be considered as a colleague you might consult when feeling stuck, or unsure where to go. The specific therapy tools provided are what

I have found work for me, but they may not work for you. The most important part of working effectively with young people with cancer is learning the language and then making it your own, so that those skills you have are translatable to cancer-related issues.

## A word about therapies...

Throughout this book you will find a combination of therapy techniques that are mostly based around Acceptance and Commitment therapy (ACT), Cognitive Behavioural therapy (CBT) and ideas around existentialism. There will not be a detailed explanation about any of the theory or specifics underpinning these therapies as it is assumed that if you are reading this book, you will already have a good working understanding of the appropriate therapeutic techniques of working with young people. If this is not the case, I would recommend reading some of the many reputable works on these therapeutic techniques.

It is worth noting, however, that there are some therapeutic modalities that lend themselves naturally to working with young people with cancer. This is particularly the case for Acceptance and Commitment therapy, especially when considering that most of the young people in this situation will find themselves in situations that are not 'fixable'[*] and the worries and fears they find spinning in their heads are based strongly in the possibility of reality. For this reason, teaching young people to work with their thoughts is a much more effective strategy than trying to teach them to simply 'get rid of them' or 'challenge them' out of existence. It is not that traditional cognitive and behavioural are unhelpful or

---

[*] In the sense that at the time of treatment or completion of treatment, they are in a situation where they ultimately have little or no control.

useless in this setting, instead, the opposite is true. Some of these methods underpin the management of the day-to-day minutiae of treatment, long hospital admissions, anticipatory nausea and vomiting, as well as contemplating making sense of the future where cancer is an integral part.

When working with young people the specifics of the therapeutic techniques often become less important than the engagement itself. This does not mean, of course, that you should abandon all the functional therapy and follow the whim that is in the room. The rules you might employ with other groups will feel helpful, however, there may be several differences in the ways that these strategies are employed. For instance, it is not uncommon in therapy sessions with young people in this context to use multiple techniques, perhaps oscillating between various strategies to find a good fit. This may feel disingenuous as a therapist, however, and against all the strict training received around building a good intervention.

Sometimes with young people you will find yourself in the space where the therapy may not have a discernible direction, and the space will be more powerful than the therapeutic techniques that got you there. This therapeutic space is the product of building a strong relationship with a young person over many months (or sometimes even years), and is a privileged and honourable place to sit in, even when it feels difficult for you as a therapist.

# Chapter 1

# Introduction to a Cancer Diagnosis

'And then he told me I had cancer. Fucking awesome.'
— 19-year-old.

Undeniably, a cancer diagnosis in the critical period of adolescence or young adulthood is going to have a significant impact on wellbeing and mental health, not just at the time of diagnosis, but throughout the remainder of a young person's life. Often, young people who have lived through a cancer experience will speak fondly of the positive impact that it has on their sense of self; however, this is often accompanied by a significant contrast of suffering, distress and worry about the cancer. Following a diagnosis, the cancer is an ever-present thread, moving and changing over time. The process of diagnosis, treatment and survivorship provides unique challenges that separate a young person from others around them — including their peers, arguably the most important group. The cost of the cancer is significant, but often for young people they manage it with humour, skills and resilience that health professionals may underestimate.

There can be the assumption that the cancer appears as if from nowhere, which for some of the cancers this may be the case, for instance, those with acute leukaemias. However, for some young patients the journey to diagnosis has may have been long and drawn out, which may build some distrust of the medical system and frustrations at feeling that they aren't being heard. For instance, among young people with bone tumours, the process of having symptoms recognised and identified as cancer may take months. In these situations, young people often indicate that they feel that they aren't being listened to, or that the medical contacts they have dealt with have been quite dismissive of their experience.

Cancer in this population usually comes as an incredible shock and generally, families and young people will report a sense of comfort from being in the care of a tertiary service, and will often talk about the comfort of knowing that there is a plan. Something is going to be done — even if the things that will be done, for example, chemotherapy, surgery or radiotherapy, are inherently quite uncertain and provide fear in themselves. For young people who have had a delay in diagnosis, once they have been initiated into the tertiary service they feel that things start to move very quickly, and before they know it, they have been whisked into surgery, started chemotherapy, and have not really had time to process the enormity of what it means to have to cancer.

### The Time of Diagnosis

Psychologically, young people will often present as quite calm at diagnosis and in the weeks following. There appears to be something adaptive about being able to 'go onto autopilot' and just do what needs to be done and not be too present or engaged about the impact long term, or in some instances even in the shorter term of what the cancer might mean. In those initial stages of diagnosis and treatment, the focus is more on experiencing each beginning stage of each new treatment. For instance, getting caught in the anxiety and trying to understand what it means to have chemotherapy starting, or what it will feel like for surgery to happen, rather than a specific focus on managing the impact of the cancer itself. For the most part, these natural tendencies to go into 'action mode' assist young people to get on with what needs to be done, and to not question too much the 'existential' impact of the diagnosis. These strategies free up space to make decisions about treatment, surviving the treatment itself psychologically, and building resilience for challenging situations (such as being in hospital for long periods of time). Initially, on diagnosis and in the weeks following, young people describe a sense of disconnection between the knowledge of the diagnosis and the reality of it.

When speaking with young people before they start treatment, they can generally acknowledge this disconnection and anticipate that this feeling will not be sustainable or prolonged. In most situations, the disconnection dissipates at the commencement of treatment, with the physical impact of the treatments reconnecting the young person with the reality of the situation. An exception to this, of course, is young people who have been unwell for extended periods of time, and who present as physically very unwell. They will often indicate that the time taken to diagnosis is the most difficult to manage, and find the commencement of treatment quite reassuring and comforting, albeit with some elements of anxiety.

Most young people have had limited exposure to the reality of hospital and treatment. If they have known people who have had treatment, or been unwell, it is likely those people were considerably older and the regimes of treatment looked very different to their own experience of the intense and all-consuming treatment protocols in which young people will be engaged. The initial tolerance for hospital for most young people will be quite good, but as the days and weeks roll on, with little novelty or distraction, and the reality of sharing a ward (often with people who are much older or sicker than themselves), this tolerance will deteriorate. It is common for young people to become anxious and distressed about having to manage the long stretches of time in the wards, with much uncertainty, particularly in the context of white cell recovery (a side effect of chemotherapy), or back-to -back cycles of treatment, which occur mostly in the haematological malignancies.

Health professionals make a consistent and concerted effort to explain the risk and realities of treatment to patients; however, just as consistently the response from patients following the first cycle of treatment, or in recovery from surgery, is 'I didn't know that it was going to be this bad!' or 'No one told me about this'. There are many protocols and approaches in place to make sure that young people and their families get all pertinent information, but evidently it appears that even with the information provided, this knowledge is not synthesised in a way that helps manage the outcome of treatments. There could be several reasons for this, including the general sense of infallibility for younger patients as a function of age and experience. There is also the limited understanding of anyone who has not been exposed to something, for instance, trying to explain the sensation of going in a plane, without having ever been in a plane. Young patients, in fact all patients, have limited capacity to take on large amounts of information at the time of diagnosis, which is often when they are given a lot of written brochures and resources. For young people drip-feeding information is a more effective strategy that allows them to take on small pieces of information and come back to you with questions when they have had time to process things. Families may appear to be the opposite to the young person, and be looking for information everywhere, including the internet. It is reasonable to assume that young people and their families will search the name of their disease, and the words 'life expectancy' or some variation of, and with most cancers almost all searches will uncover the word 'death' in the first couple of results. For this reason, and to help give a sense of a plan for the young person, there is a benefit in having very clear expectations about what their treatment will look like. Having a protocol document that can be given to young people and their families to let them know what is going to happen at each stage, and who will be involved in their care.

## Meeting a Young Person at Diagnosis

Whether it be on the ward, or in an outpatient setting, if you are meeting a young person and their family within 72 hours of their diagnosis they are unlikely to be able to process much of what you will have to say, or give you much input about how they perceive the diagnosis itself. As mentioned previously, young people are often in the space of feeling particularly detached about the situation at this time, and will not have had time to process much of what is going on. The goal of early meetings with a young person and their family should be about relationship and introduction rather than assessment and providing information. Then, as they start to process the information and become aware of the significance of the impact of treatment, there will already be a context to your relationship and you will be able to help them manage this. It is generally only clinicians working in acute care facilities who will meet young people around this time of diagnosis, with many patients seeking support in the community following diagnosis and treatment, and generally when they are re-joining their peer group and 'getting back to normal' (see the survivorship section on page 108). Even if working in the community, it is important to understand the processes that young people go through psychologically and emotionally with the treatment process to allow you to support them through its ramifications.

# Chapter 2

# Chemotherapy

'That whole first cycle was spent tuned into my body, just waiting for it all to go to shit.'
— 17-year-old male

Chemotherapy is made up of drugs which destroy cancer cells and can cause significant side effects to patients including nausea and vomiting, gastrointestinal issues, fatigue, hair loss, increased risk of infection as well as others (Cancer Council NSW, 2016). These medications can be given intravenously (through a drip), orally, directly into tissues or organs or as a cream (Cancer Council NSW, 2016). Sometimes people will have one drug only, but in young people it is common that they will receive a combination of chemotherapy drugs at once.

Most young people diagnosed with cancer are likely to have some form of intravenous chemotherapy. There are some exceptions to this, for instance those who have been diagnosed with bone tumours manageable by resection only or some skin cancers. Chemotherapy is a difficult process for most patients, and often young people report feeling quite curious and anxious to start therapy, particularly those who have extended delays in diagnosis or for those who are unwell.Generally, prior to starting the first treatment cycle young people will present as feeling quite calm, but may have many questions and concerns about how the chemotherapy itself will work, as well as what is likely to happen to them. They will often identify with someone else that they have known who has had chemotherapy, and try and project forward as to how their experience may be similar. Expectedly, for that first cycle, the psychological burden of anxiety is high, as with every symptom or sensation within their bodies the young people are often trying to anticipate the significance of such, and whether they need to be concerned.

As patients move into the second treatment cycle, generally one of two things will happen. They will report that the treatment had been much more manageable than they had been anticipating and they will feel that they can tolerate further cycles well. Conversely, and much more difficult to manage, are the patients who had either been anticipating that chemotherapy would be easy and found the first cycle much more difficult than they had thought it would be, or those who had a particularly difficult time with side effects in the first cycle. For this latter group of patients, they are likely to experience significant anxiety, avoidance behaviours and anticipatory nausea and vomiting as a result of their early experiences. For this reason, it is particularly important that young people have good symptom control in the first cycle, including specific education about when to use their anti-nausea medications, and when to engage the support of their care team. A low-symptomatic first chemotherapy cycle can prevent difficulties in managing future cycles, particularly in those young people who are already quite anxious.

For almost all patients, regardless of whether they have a high side-effect burden, most young people will have a significant 'crash' around the third or fourth cycle of treatment. This event is characterised by low mood, a sense of hopelessness, ambivalence about continuing treatment, reduced engagement with their health care team and some withdrawal from peers. Generally, young people will speak about a frustration with the 'ongoingness' of the treatment, and a sense that they have lost 'their lives' to chemotherapy, as they remain focused and fixated on the details of having routine and predictable cycles of chemotherapy. This can be particularly exacerbated in patients who have had multiple complications/admissions between cycles, including relating to febrile neutropenia*, with patients having little time away from the hospital system. This period of low mood is often self-limiting, with patients being buoyed by mid-treatment scan results, or finding that they have passed the halfway mark through their treatment. However, when these mood symptoms are occurring they can be quite reluctant to engage in support, which is one of the key reasons for engaging them early in diagnosis [see dialogue box 1]. For patients particularly affected by changes in mood, these may continue in varying degrees through the remainder of their treatment, and can worsen towards the penultimate cycles of treatment.

> 'I am so close now, but I still have to have another 2 full cycles before I make it to the end.'
> — 16-year-old male

For young people in their final cycle of treatment, they often have mixed and uncertain feelings. Some may become elated at the sense of having 'finished' and they can manage throughout the final cycle psychologically quite well. However, others can become highly anxious and worried about the next steps, and what it will mean to finish treatment. Young people will identify that as they get closer to the end of treatment, there is more pressure applied by those around them to celebrate and declare that they have 'beaten' cancer, when they can feel quite distressed by the idea of what finishing treatment might mean. Summarised in Table 2.1 is what to expect from patients emotionally in the context of their chemotherapy treatment.

---

\* Febrile neutropenia is the development of fever, often with other signs of infection, in a patient with an abnormally low number of white blood cells.

## Table 2.1

| Cycle Number | Possible Psychological Reactions | Management Strategies |
|---|---|---|
| 1 | • Acute anxiety in the context of being uncertain of side effects/impact of chemotherapy<br>• Ambivalence/Disconnection<br>• Reports that they are feeling 'ok' about it, and it just needs to be done.<br>• Excitement/Relief about starting | • Psycho-education about the treatment itself and what to expect. However, it is important that this information be kept quite light, and not overwhelming (remembering that when patients are anxious their cognitive processing and ability to manage information is quite low).<br>• Specific strategies around particular thoughts and worries.<br>• Validation and reassurance |
| 2 | • Ongoing anxiety about the treatment, but also new anxieties about becoming unwell again.<br>• Avoidance<br>• Anticipatory Anxiety | • Ongoing Anxiety Management strategies<br>• Specific strategies for managing anticipatory anxiety (see chapter 12) |
| 3–4 | • Ongoing anxiety/Anticipatory Anxiety<br>• Depression/Low Mood | • Mood management<br>• Anxiety Management |
| 4+ | • Ambivalence<br>• Ongoing Anxiety/Low Mood<br>• Frustration | • Ongoing Mood and Anxiety management<br>• Frustration tolerance |
| Final Cycle | • Fear/Uncertainty<br>• Excitement<br>• Apprehension | • Preparation for survivorship |

## Strategies to Manage Difficulties with Treatment

There are various strategies which need to be employed during the chemotherapy treatment phase. These may vary from cycle to cycle, as well as in the context of changes in medical status, the impact of medications and the difficulties in managing peers/relationships/external stressors. Table 2.1 shows the types of interventions that are appropriate and helpful for young people as they move through the stages of treatment. These will be explained further below.

### Psycho-Education

Early in the chemotherapy process it is particularly important to provide comprehensive psycho-education for young people around what to expect from their treatment, including physical and psychological side effects and examples of how other young people have managed or coped with symptoms. This is important in the context of regimes where young people have medications or chemotherapy drugs that are likely to cause changes in their mood (see chapter 6 on medications). Often by providing psycho-education early, there is capacity to educate young people about potential side effects and symptoms so that they are able to have a reference point should they be affected in the future. Furthermore, it is helpful to pre-empt the potential for changes in mood and changes to the emotional reactions that happen over time.

### Anxiety Management

There may be many facets of anxiety management required for young people undergoing chemotherapy, and these may change from cycle to cycle. Generally, prior to the initial treatment cycle young people's anxiety is focused on the potential outcomes of the treatment, and fear around how this may emerge. This is even more pronounced in young people who have difficulty with medical procedures or medical anxiety (see chapter 17 on anticipatory nausea and vomiting). It is normal and some will elect to minimise the potential worry about this, whereas others will become fixated on those potential outcomes. For the following cycles, the focus on anxiety management will often be based around the anticipatory nature of the chemotherapy nausea and trying to avoid situations that become triggers. Generally, as patients get closer to the end of treatment, the anxiety focus can shift to anticipating what may happen at the end of treatment, or anxiety about whether the treatment has been effective.

There is no catch-all approach for managing young people's anxiety at this time, as each particular 'type' may require considerably different interventions. For instance, the interventions for anticipatory anxiety will look very different for those who are anxious about what their scan results may show. Generally, ACT-based strategies work well as they can promote working with the situation individuals are faced with (and that is unlikely to change), and gaining strategies to cope with it, rather than engaging in discussion about how the situation could be different. For some young people, the anxiety about chemotherapy becomes so significant that it can impair their ability to complete treatment. For these patients, medications may become the most effective management tool (particularly in the case of anticipatory anxiety).

### Mood Management

As outlined above, it is common for young people to experience considerable mood change in the context of their treatment. This is multifactorial in nature, particularly in those who have significant side effects or fatigue following treatment, and may be mediated by the medications themselves, including steroids (see chapter 6 on medication effects). For most patients, boredom, frustration, discomfort and isolation become features of low mood, which will often become evident around the third cycle of treatment. It is around this time that the novelty of treatment has passed, and the support that was initially strong may have faded somewhat. This is also the time when the true unrelenting nature of the reality of treatment becomes evident, and the sensation of being 'trapped' by the cancer can feel very real.

The severity of the mood changes at this time can be variable. For some, they may mention in passing that they are feeling particularly bored or 'over' chemotherapy, whereas for others there will be a marked change in affect, engagement and cognition. Obviously, this severity will dictate the level of appropriate intervention. For those who have mild changes, often engagement in behavioural strategies including fatigue management, activation and pleasure/achievement scheduling can bolster them through this time. Those with more significant changes will generally require more significant intervention, including a structured mood management program and, at times, medication if the changes are sustained for more than two weeks.

At this time, young people generally respond well to strategies focused on providing a solution to how they are feeling; for instance, focusing on the things that they can do to help them feel better in the context of treatment, managing their fatigue and how they can maximise the time between cycles when they feel better. A key element of these interventions is working with the medical team to ensure that all the medical issues are being managed, and that the mood change is not a result of a medication, or an underlying disease process. In addition, engagement around the underlying fears, thoughts and concerns can provide a powerful space for young people to discuss and challenge their perceptions and existential distress around cancer and the impact of the treatment.

### Preparation for Survivorship

The perception of completion of treatment for many young people and those around them is often one of idealism and relief. However, it is well established that most people completing cancer treatment can find it overwhelming and a time filled with anxiety and uncertainty. In the lead-up to the final cycles of treatment, the reality of being 'off' treatment and the inherent uncertainty can become anxiety provoking and difficult. It is at this time that it can be helpful to start talking about what to expect in the survivorship phase, and to encourage young people to think about how they may manage the emotions emerging at this time. Mostly, young people are very open to this as they have been finding these thoughts and worries difficult to manage, and are able to engage in proactive strategies to help.

# Chapter 3

# Radiotherapy

Radiotherapy is the use of x-rays to shrink or destroy cancer cells, and stop them multiplying, sometimes used by itself, but often with other treatments like chemotherapy, hormone therapies or surgery (Cancer Council NSW, 2016). The side effects of radiotherapy are very dependent on the site of the treatment, but many patients describe some fatigue, and skin irritation (Cancer Council NSW, 2016). Courses of treatment can go for varying amounts of time depending on the site and dose of treatment (Cancer Council NSW, 2016).

Most patients describe radiotherapy as quite tolerable in comparison to chemotherapy. This is, of course, dependent on the area having radiotherapy and the organs affected. Many patients have conjured up painful and traumatic images about what the radiotherapy might look like, generally based on movies or books, and are pleasantly surprised to hear that radiotherapy is quite similar to an X-ray, and for the most part is painless.

Despite its general tolerability, however, there are several situations which can provide young people with significant difficulties in managing radiotherapy and its side effects. These include:

- treatment for tumours in the head and neck region
- treatment targeting the gastrointestinal region
- the ongoing nature of the treatment.

## Treatment for Tumours in the Head and Neck Region

There are several aspects of treatment targeting the head and neck area which impact on a young person's psychological wellbeing. This becomes particularly evident for those who are having local treatment for a head and neck tumour (i.e. throat, larynx or tongue). The treatment for these tumours generally leads to significant side effects including pain, difficulty with swallowing and eating, use of secondary feeding devices (such as a tube inserted directly into the stomach called a PEG) as well as daily treatment requiring a mask. For these patients, the impact is multifactorial and may change as they progress through treatment. This can also be influenced by them gaining external information, particularly from the internet, about 'how bad' the head and neck treatment can be. Furthermore, the process of head and neck treatment is generally unpleasant, and has far-reaching consequences on young people during this time. For instance, the insertion of a PEG tube to allow for nutrition to continue when they become unable to eat because of treatment has significant impacts on body image, further compounded by changes in the skin around the radiotherapy site. The pain and fatigue caused either by the radiotherapy or the tumour itself leads to decreased tolerance overall, and can mean that a young person who would generally manage well may become frustrated, anxious, overwhelmed or avoidant of treatment. Each of these factors need to be managed in turn, all the while being mindful of the larger context and surrounding complications.

For most people, the need to have a special radiotherapy mask fitted and used for their radiotherapy treatment can be quite unpleasant, however, for those who are claustrophobic and anxious this becomes almost impossible to manage. It is not uncommon for head and neck protocols to have up to six weeks of daily radiotherapy, which is traumatic for those who are claustrophobic and needing daily exposure to the mask. Often patients who have difficulties managing the mask and the claustrophobia associated with it may require intensive exposure and graded hierarchy programs to simply get them through the treatment cycle. This becomes particularly difficult if they experience local swelling as the result of treatment itself that makes the mask feel tighter and perpetuates the sense of feeling trapped. Unfortunately, for some patients, the extent of their claustrophobia does not get identified prior to the initial fitting of the mask and radiotherapy planning, which may lead to referral after 'flooding' has already occurred. This requires significant intervention to allow the young person to proceed with treatment. To work with young people around this requires specialist and planned intervention It also needs to include the radiation oncologist and radiation therapist to ensure that each day's treatment has a predictable and manageable course for the patient, and does not inadvertently further traumatise, or undo any anxiety management strategies that have been put in place. As for other unmanageable anxiety in the context of treatment, in some cases it is advisable to engage support from a psychiatrist about the appropriateness of using an anxiolytic to help the young person complete treatment.

## Treatment Targeting the Gastrointestinal Region

The impact of treatment to the gastrointestinal region is not so much based on psychological factors, but rather on physical factors of treatment that can produce substantial difficulties in managing psychologically. It is not uncommon for patients who are having radiotherapy to a section of their gastrointestinal system to have significant side effects including nausea, diarrhoea, vomiting or constipation. All these symptoms are manageable, but can have a strong psychological impact on the mood of a young patient, particularly if they are unable to continue to do their normal activities due to the above.

## Ongoing Nature of the Treatment

One of the biggest challenges for patients undergoing radiotherapy is related to the unrelenting nature of the treatment. For most patients, their treatment cycles will last at least five weeks, and they will be required to attend the hospital daily throughout this time. Although the treatment itself is relatively quick (usually finished in fifteen minutes), young people often find daily attendance at the hospital draining and difficult to manage. For many, they will be able to organise their radiotherapy around the other aspects of their lives, such as study or work. However, others will be unable to do so and radiotherapy can be seen as a difficult and obstructive part of their daily lives, which is even more pronounced in patients that are finding treatment itself hard to manage, or having significant side effects.

When working with young people around these frustrations, there is often a double-pronged approach required. Firstly, by focusing on any underlying psychological distress or concerns, for instance anxiety about treatment, claustrophobia or body image. Secondly, working with the young person to manage the scheduling of radiotherapy to help bolster their mood in the context of its ongoing nature. This is particularly important in those patients who are unable to return to their normal activities, where there is a risk that the attendance at the hospital each day becomes the focus, and at times is an anxiety trigger for their entire day. Gentle encouragement towards behavioural activities to help make use of their time is often helpful, but it is worth noting that these activities often need to be very easy in nature due to the other physical issues which are occurring concurrently. This can also be helpful for those patients who have returned to commitments and are balancing radiotherapy with work or study. Often as treatment progresses, fatigue can become cumulative and young people can become overwhelmed as they try and balance all aspects of their lives and, as such, often respond well to strategies to help manage energy conservation and pacing.

# Chapter 4

# Surgery

'And I woke up and everything below my knee was gone. I knew that's what was going to happen, but it didn't really make sense until it happened.'
— 23-year-old male

Most young people will require some form of surgery during their cancer experience. These can vary from relatively simple procedures (insertion of an access device) to long and complex surgeries, for instance, removal of a pelvic tumour. Most young people will be naïve to surgery outside of their cancer, and are generally quite anxious and worried about the potential outcomes and risks.

Many young people will have had a biopsy prior to diagnosis, the exceptions generally being those diagnosed with acute leukaemia. There is often an identification that the time of the biopsy is the start of the cancer journey, and young people will often refer to that time as being quite anxiety provoking and overwhelming. Thankfully, most biopsies are very simple procedures and medically straightforward, so the anxiety that the young person expresses is related to the uncertainty about the results, rather than the procedure itself. That said, the biopsy may be the first time that a young person has ever been exposed to anaesthetics, which can be overwhelming in itself. It can be difficult for a young person to conceptualise the idea that they can simply not be present for a period of time.

For larger surgeries, there are generally more anxieties and uncertainty, as well as a greater awareness of their implications. Young people will often report a sense of feeling unprepared for the reality of what they face after their surgery, and the impact on their recovery. There are several factors why young people find it hard to make sense of this. Firstly, despite very high-resolution scanning and technology the exact extent of surgery is often unclear until the surgeons have examined the site itself. Young people will be given a set of parameters and options that may happen, but are dependent on what the surgeons see when they 'go in', which means young people won't know exactly what has happened until they wake up. Secondly, even when a young person is provided with exact details about the surgery, they will often not be able to conceptualise what the outcome of that means in a functional sense.

> 'They told me that were going to take the nerves, but I thought that my leg would still do things. It doesn't. It's completely useless.'
> —24-year-old female

In some ways, this strategy is protective on the part of the young person. It allows them to make decisions about having quite overwhelming and horrible surgeries while remaining hopeful and optimistic that they may not be as adversely affected as their surgeons have described. However, this can result in a difficult postsurgical recovery as they try and reconceptualise what their world will look like with the changes and the loss of function that may have occurred. Consider the case of Peter below:

> Peter is a 15-year-old male with a large sacral tumour. He has had chemotherapy, and is now due to have surgery to remove the affected bone and have his pelvis reconstructed. He is likely to have a long recovery with at least six weeks in hospital on bed rest, and months of rehabilitation following such. He has been an avid sports person all his life and has

heard that he will be unable to do any of the sports that he has done previously, but reports that he has read on the internet that someone has had a similar surgery was able to return to playing rugby following recovery. Peter is also optimistic that the surgeons will be able to preserve his sexual, as well as bladder and bowel function. He has also spoken to the surgeon about how long he will need to be in hospital. The surgeon mentioned that the fastest that anyone has gotten out of hospital is four weeks, and Peter is convinced that he will be able to beat that!

Young people such as Peter will often feel a sense of optimism about how quickly they will be able to get out of hospital, and can minimise the reality of what their postsurgery recovery will look like. There is no value in taking away that optimism or sense of hope from young people, in fact the opposite is true. However, it is of paramount importance that young people have appropriate guidelines on which to base their expectations. It is far more psychologically helpful for young people to be given the worst-case scenario (particularly related to how long they are likely to stay in hospital) to adjust to. It is likely that they will do better than the worst-case scenario and be buoyed by their progress earlier than expected. This is a much better psychological space for a young person to be in than where they set expectations for a certain date or for particular schedule only to be devastated and despairing when this does not occur. This approach, of course, can be somewhat contentious within the medical community, where the sense of maintaining positivity and hope for patients can often be seen as the driving factor, rather than its implications.

For patients such as Peter, the long stays in hospital with limited ability to move or change position can become a significant factor in their capacity to cope. For anyone, being 'stuck' in bed for up to six weeks without the ability to sit up, get out of bed or move will very reasonably have an impact on their mood and ability to function. In the process of this normal adjustment, young people will often disengage from activities and care providers, which is not concerning as long as they can identify that they will feel better when things change, or when they make progress. If young people are well engaged with clinicians, it allows a discussion and plan to occur prior to these low periods of mood occurring, and allows for a reference point for patients to recall. It is easy to draw on strategies that you have identified with the young person in the past to help them reconnect with what they can do to manage what is happening for them this time.

The postsurgery realisation for patients that their function has changed significantly can have a very detrimental effect on mood and perceptions of coping. This is particularly true for patients who have been resistant to discuss or conceptualise the impact of their surgery, or who thought that they would be the patient who would 'beat the odds'. For these patients, the initial reality of waking up to a disfigured, or dysfunctional limb or body part, and the rehabilitation that follows becomes quite confronting. It is common for young people to disconnect from the rehabilitation process, or express a sense of hopelessness about the future in the context of things 'never being the same again'. When this process is coupled with significant pain following surgery, young people will often become quite flat in mood and despairing, which can be alleviated most effectively by the young person themselves seeing progress and improvement in their coping and function.

Patients can be well acquainted with pain prior to their surgery and, as such, may be well versed in managing the surgical pain, and can distinguish this from cancer pain itself. Most people can articulate a separateness about these types of pain and, as such, the surgical pain is often less distressing as there is a sense that it can be managed well. The exceptions to this can be related to the type of pain itself, for instance those who have been left with significant nerve pain, or pain from phantom limbs. Not surprisingly, patients generally have quite low tolerance to managing this type of pain and will have difficulty managing their mood, particularly if it is ongoing or unlikely to be well managed.

Just as certain surgeries have more impact on function than others, some will have significant impacts on body image and sense of self than others. There are obvious times when it would be expected that a young person would have difficulty adjusting to surgical changes, for instance, a young woman having a double mastectomy, or a young person having a leg or arm amputated. There can often be 'hidden' surgery impacts that are devastating in their impact on body image and function, and both the medical teams and the young people themselves might be reluctant to talk about these things. For instance, surgeries for colorectal cancer can often result in the creation of a stoma, which may be temporary or permanent, and will have obvious implications on the young person's identity and sexuality. The adaptation to a stoma will often take many months, in which time the young person may be very reluctant to engage with their partner sexually, or to engage in any intimate contact. This is particularly difficult for young people who are single, who are worried about the change in their bodies for finding a new partner, and how they will explain their stoma, amputation, scarring or cancer experience in general (see chapter 8 on relationships).

Below is a summary of strategies and tips for helping a young person engage in preparation and management of surgery.

## Table 4.1

| Time frame | Strategies to help manage |
| --- | --- |
| Pre Surgery | • Engaging the young person in discussions about decision making, and understanding the surgery and what it will mean for their function |
| | • Psycho-education around managing long admissions (particularly important for young people who have not had much time in hospital). |
| | • Normalisation of anxiety and apprehension in the lead up to the surgery |
| | • Strategies around managing pain in the post-surgical period and education around what to expect in the immediate time after surgery |
| In the days following surgery | The young person may be unable to engage with the clinician themselves, but you may be able to assist the patients support people through psycho-education about normal and expected reactions at this time. |
| During the inpatient stay | • Strategies around adjusting to life in the hospital environment, and support in coping with frustration in this context |
| | • Support in managing the implications of surgery, or difficulty in managing expectations around recovery (for instance frustrations about not progressing as fast as they would like) |
| | • Advocating on behalf of the young person to teams if they are having difficulties in managing practical concerns such as repeated cannulations, confronting |

patients within the ward setting, difficulty gaining information from the teams.

- Strategies for sleep management, and sleep hygiene, including engaging teams around the use of sleep aids.

- Encouragement of young people to remain engaged with their peers and strategies to help facilitate such.

- Ongoing interventions for anxiety or changes in mood.

- Preparedness psychologically to returning 'home' and the implications of what they may mean for them in the context of surgery.

| | |
|---|---|
| If a young person is to have chemotherapy whilst still in hospital recovering from surgery | • Engagement of strategies which are useful for managing chemotherapy outside of the hospital.<br><br>• Allowing the young person to have permission to have a period of low mood in the context of the chemotherapy. This is very common if patients are to have chemotherapy in this setting, particularly for those who are bed bound. It is important that this is normalised and anticipated, so that patients are able to have a framework for such.<br><br>• Implementation of self-care strategies which help bolster their mood, including particular foods, items from home or visits from particular people. |
| Following discharge | • Ongoing engagement and assessment around mood changes (this is particularly important on return home, as patients will often have a period of feeling quite |

flat and despairing when the reality of the impact of the surgery becomes clear in their own environment).

- Psychological preparedness around managing expectations of self and others in the context of their recovery period

- Strategies to manage adaptation to permanent disability.

# Chapter 5

# Stem Cell Transplants

A Stem cell transplant is the process of replacing the cells in the body that make blood, and is usually performed in those with haematological malignancies (like leukaemia) or high risk solid tumours. This occurs by giving high dose chemotherapy and radiotherapy, followed by an infusion of the persons own stem cells (autologous transplant) or cells from someone else that are matched to the patient (allogenic transplant)(Leukaemia Foundation, 2017). Allogenic transplants carry much more short and long term risk than those who are able to have a transplant from their own cells (Leukaemia Foundation, 2017).

Stem cell transplants are among the riskiest procedures that can be offered to young people, although over time it is becoming less so. For most, the concept of a transplant is enough to induce significant anxiety and worry, without the further aspects of long admissions, uncertain medical outcomes, significant risk of morbidity and mortality and a long recovery. Stem cell transplant is often seen as the 'ending' of the journey for several reasons dependent on the disease state, relapse status or wellness of the young person. Not unreasonably, young people often have significant difficulties in managing the stem cell transplant process, as well as dealing with the uncertainty around the potential outcomes.

First and foremost, the decision to proceed with the transplant itself can be a difficult and stressful time. In some cases, there may be a very clear decision-making process, and the stem cell transplant will have been on the agenda since the diagnosis. Commonly, the transplant will be given as an option following relapse or poor disease response. This means that young people may be in a different headspace considering the idea of the transplant, to what they would be if the transplant had been on the agenda from the time of diagnosis. For some young people, the stem cell transplant process may be perceived as the 'treatment of last resort', which makes it inherently difficult to manage the associated decision-making process. At times, the decision will be made not to proceed with the transplant given poor prognosis and high risk, but many patients will make the decision to go ahead with the procedure, even while knowing that the risks are high. It is important that young people have a good understanding of what the transplant procedure involves, as well as having a clear understanding of the risks (which will vary for each individual case). For some, they feel that the 'only option' is going to be a reasonable option regardless of the risk, whereas for others any risk mitigates their decision to have the stem cell transplant .

Even for patients who have a clear decision-making process around their choice to have the stem cell transplant, the initial stages of starting the transplant will generally be marred by significant anxiety and uncertainty. In the weeks following their transplant many patients say that if they had known what it would be like they would have opted to not go through with it. Without appropriate support, young people can become very anxious or depressed at all stages of the transplant process, particularly while they are in the midst of the neutropenia phase (when the patient essentially has no effective immune system and is susceptible to infection), and awaiting recovery. It is common in the weeks leading up to the stem cell transplant for patients to present with a steadfast attitude and suggest that they 'just want to get on with it'. But clinicians may note increased anxiety and questioning, difficulty sleeping on the ward, or other behaviours not congruent with the young person's typical presentation. This is heightened in patients who have a long period of time in hospital prior to treatment side effects becoming evident — for instance, patients who have long protocols with premedications, or need line insertion and so forth. These patients often see other patients who are quite unwell, and others who have had transplants may provide information about what it is like. For young people who have spent a lot of time on the haematology ward, this will not be unexpected or shocking, but for solid tumour patients who have been mostly outpatients, the awareness of the 'unwellness' of the patients around them can be quite distressing. Young people will often talk about not knowing that there is a risk of mortality in the process, and there is nothing to guarantee that they will be able to live through the transplant. This can present a sense of existential distress, or a sense that they have said goodbye to everyone, and completed their 'legacy' work before coming into the ward.

> 'I have been able to have most of the cards done, there are a couple of people that will miss out if I cark it this time … but what can I do now?'
> — 19-year-old male

After treatment, most patients will talk about the infusion of their stem cells as being quite tedious and boring, especially for those who are well versed in blood transfusion. But they may find the symbolic importance of receiving the cells quite an anxiety provoking and overwhelming aspect. There is often a sense that they will be inherently changed following the day of infusion, which for the most part is accurate. This is less pronounced in those having autologous transplants, but those who received another person's bone marrow or stem cells can find this sense of 'new identity' difficult to reconcile and will often attest that if they make it through the process they will contact the donor. Understanding also that a part of them is irrevocably gone is a very difficult existential concept for anyone to take on, let alone someone who is also quite unwell following intensive therapy. Around this time, young people will generally have freedom to think a bit more than usual as they are awaiting the onslaught of the chemotherapy to 'kick in'. This can often lead to a decrease in mood, and a pensive reflection of the meaning associated with the process of the transplant.

'Well, from today, I am an American I guess. I wonder what other parts of me will be different after today.'
— 17-year-old female

For much of the transplant process, young people will be too unwell to engage in psychological therapy. Particularly those who have had allogeneic cells, as they are likely to have more significant side effects. There are several windows of time in which young people are likely to engage in work around how they are coping during the transplant and, outside of this, psychological strategies are unlikely to be particularly helpful. In the midst of the transplant young people will have limited capacity to engage with suggestions or things to help them get through the process. Often the most helpful thing that you can offer at that time is reassurance that they will be able to get through it, and that the way they feel is temporary. The caveat to this, of course, is that medical things are progressing appropriately. Patients are often given very good guides as to what is normal and what to expect in the context of their particular transplant protocol, although they may have conceptualised this differently to how it feels when it is happening to them. In these cases, it's helpful to provide gentle reminders about what they had been anticipating and identifying whether that symptom is what is happening. For instance, patients will often not equate 'mouth ulcers' with mucositis (painful inflammation and ulceration of the mucous membranes lining the digestive tract), which is very common in the process of recovery. If they are distressed about the mucositis, sometimes it is helpful to give them a context such as: 'Remember how when we were talking a couple of weeks ago about the mouth ulcers that you might get, it sounds like that's what is happening now'.

The most challenging times for young people undergoing stem cell transplant is generally after the transplant procedure's 'worst bit' has passed, and they are starting to feel well again (relatively speaking). This is the time where they are often feeling better than they had been, but are not well enough to go home. Or where they may not have had their cells fully recover, and will be getting significant 'cabin fever' from being in isolation (due to infection risk). Isolation is particularly difficult for those who are used to being able to have large groups of friends or family coming to visit when they have been in hospital. While most people will not feel like having too many people around them when they are very unwell, visitors can often provide much-needed distraction as they start to improve and feel better. Since isolation necessarily prevents young people leaving their room, the challenge of keeping themselves entertained and not feeling overwhelmed by being 'trapped' with only one visitor at a time can become a difficult mind game to play. This is particularly challenging for those who have claustrophobia, reactions to steroids (such as becoming hypomanic) or those with limited social support.

> 'I thought I would never get out again, and I started to forget that there is a world just outside of those four boxed-in walls'
> — 19-year-old female

It is at this time of the transplant when the role of the psychologist can become particularly important, often in the capacity of simply keeping the young person focused on managing their time and not becoming caught up in longing to 'escape' or dwelling on the symptoms that they have. At this time, young people are often very responsive to task setting to help time pass, as well as psycho-education for pacing and adjustment to the sense of the 'new normal' where they may not have the physical strength to do the things easily undertaken in the past. This drop in physical strength can be quite confronting for the young person who may have had limited treatment prior to the transplant, when they realise that simple tasks might start to feel insurmountable, such as sitting in a chair for a couple of hours, or being able to read a book and pay attention to it.

The further challenge that can become a factor in those who have had an allogeneic transplant is related to graft versus host disease (GVHD). GVHD is a process of the new immune system where the donor cells recognise the patient's cells as foreign and attacks them(Leukaemia Foundation, 2017). GVHD can be a signal that the transplant has worked and the graft is fighting against the body as well as the underlying disease itself. This can, however, be little consolation for patients when they realise that the transplant process doesn't end at the 21-day mark (the estimated time when the patient's white cells have sufficiently recovered from treatment), and that the reality of having to manage the transplant after-effects can be significant and overwhelming. GVHD can vary from patient to patient and through the transplant course itself and for those with severe symptoms can produce life-threatening complications and lengthy hospital admissions. These effects can also have significant body image implications for those who have skin or other visible GVHD impacts. Additionally, the process of recovery from the transplant is longer than many young patients expect. They may find themselves becoming frustrated at the long-term medications, medical appointments and uncertainty. For some there is a sense of 'suspended animation' while they wait to get their lives back after the transplant is done, with the knowledge that they cannot do anything to speed up the process, and it will just take as long as it will take to recover, while also knowing that some aspects might never recover.

# Chapter 6

# Psychological Impact of Medications

Some of the most significant side effects for young people come from the medications routinely used in conjunction with chemotherapy. It important when working with young people to understand these medications and their side effects so that you can help them manage the impact they have.

### Corticosteroids — Dexamethasone, Prednisone, Prednisolone, Cortisone

The use of corticosteroids (steroids) is common in many types of tumours and treatments for most of the diseases that young people are likely to encounter. Steroids are used to manage the disease itself (for instance, haematological disorders), side effects of chemotherapy (including nausea), swelling (pain relief, brain tumours), and to increase appetite and energy.

For young people, the impact of steroids is often significant and can be quite unexpected. The steroids have a psycho-active effect that can result in significant mood and behavioural changes coexisting while the person is taking them, but also when completing the course of medication. The impact of the steroids can be related to a high dose or sensitivity to even small doses can result in considerable behavioural changes.

The most common feelings and effects that steroids have on young people can include:

- feeling energised and elated;

- increased irritability;
- flat mood and affect;
- sleep disturbance;
- increased appetite;
- gastrointestinal symptoms (including heartburn).

Although the effects listed above may appear quite innocuous in isolation, but when they are paired with the pain and discomfort of feeling considerably unwell they become more significant.

> 'Coming off the steroids was the worst. I felt awesome when I was on them, and then when I came off, I just wanted to kill myself. No one told me that would happen.'
> — 19-year-old male

Although within the oncology community there is a significant awareness of the impact of steroids, they are often overshadowed by larger concerns around more invasive treatments, the underlying disease and more toxic drugs. Generally, a young person will have some awareness of the steroids, but the warning signs of their high impact are often not retained or highlighted by the young person. This can result in young people trying to manage the symptoms in silence, and not being aware that things can be done to help them. This becomes particularly concerning in those patients who develop significant mood change, including symptoms of hypomania, significant depression, suicidal ideation or sustained insomnia. These patients are at high risk and often show significantly impaired insight into their actions, behaviours and thoughts.

> 'They made me feel like I was going crazy. I didn't realise it was the drugs, I thought it was me.'
> — 22-year-old female

At the milder end of the spectrum the effects of steroids can often be managed simply by providing a knowledge framework for patients and behavioural strategies to manage the impact of the symptoms itself.

However, for more significant steroid effects, including the management of hypomania and significant mood disturbance, the young person may need medication and management by a psychiatrist, particularly when they may require ongoing or large amounts of steroid in the future. While mood changes are common with steroids, the severity of such changes needs to be accurately assessed to ensure that the young person is not at risk of self-harm or significant mood deterioration.

Following is a summary of strategies and tips for helping a young person deal with the effects of steroid treatments.

| Reason for Steriod use | Likely Symptoms | Management Strategies |
|---|---|---|
| Anti–nausea with chemotherapy<br><br>For support in managing low energy/low appetite<br><br>Post BMT maintenance | • Increased energy<br><br>• Increased appetite<br><br>• Some sleep disturbance<br><br>• Slight changes to frustration tolerance | • For patients using relatively low doses of steroid are unlikely to have significant side effects, the most commonly reported are around increased appetite and change in sleep. However, if a young person is particularly sensitive, they can have significant mood fluctuations even on low doses.<br><br>• Providing Psycho-education to support the young person around the expectations of what may occur can be helpful. |

39

- For patients using relatively low doses of steroid are unlikely to have significant side effects, the most commonly reported are around increased appetite and change in sleep. However, if a young person is particularly sensitive, they can have significant mood fluctuations even on low doses.

- Providing Psycho-education to support the young person around the expectations of what may occur can be helpful.

- Psychological preparation for possibility of mood change coming off the medication, i.e. feeling flat or down for a couple of days, and who to contact if this is more severe, or persists longer than expected.

- Sleep hygiene strategies, including setting expectations that they are likely to have trouble to have sleeping in the days following administration (particularly if IV)

- For some patients the appetite increase can be distressing, and as such, if they are likely to be on the medication for a long time they may need support from a dietician to manage their food intake.

| Tumour specific management — for those with brain tumours, acute haematological malignancies where steroids form an active component of treatment | • Increased energy<br><br>• Significant changes in appetite<br><br>• Significant sleep disturbance<br><br>• Significant mood change which may include irritability, hypomania, steroid induced psychosis, low frustration tolerance, disinhibition whilst on the medications, and significant 'mood crash' on coming off the drug which can include suicidal ideation | • Psychological preparation for the impact of steroids, and how they are likely to feel on commencing and stopping the medications.<br><br>• Ongoing and regular mood assessment and strategies to help manage the side effects, for instance some patients find that on the 'steroid days' the best option is for them to isolate themselves, or to do something physically active to 'burn off' some of the effects.<br><br>• Support in sleep maintenance, which may require medication<br><br>• Review by Psychiatry if patient has significant changes in mood, as steroid induced mood changes can become a medical emergency.<br><br>• Engaging family members to monitor mood as the young people may have limited awareness of their mood/behaviours due to the steroids themselves. |

## Hormone Treatment

In the context of chemotherapy, it is increasingly common for young women to undertake measures for ovarian protection in an attempt to protect their fertility from the impacts of treatment. In addition, for those young people who have egg harvesting prior to the commencement of treatment there can be significant mood changes and psychological impacts from the hormone treatment itself.

Although young people will often manage the impacts of these treatments relatively well, as they are able to attribute the side effects easily to the medications and hormones, they can still have difficulty managing mood swings. In the context of both egg harvesting and ovarian protection, young people are able to identify the temporary nature of these difficulties and, as such, often adapt a 'grin and bear it' attitude to managing the hormonal side effects. For young women, or for those who have not had much exposure to gynaecological procedures, the procedures themselves can be very confronting, which, coupled with significant decision-making about their future fertility options, can be quite overwhelming.

Most young people will respond well to simple reassurance that the mood changes they are experiencing are due to the hormonal intervention and will pass once treatment ceases. This allows them to put a framework around the time and extent of their symptom management, unlike other effects and impacts of their cancer. This reassurance can often make the problem itself feel inherently more manageable. It can be helpful at this stage to provide them with practical strategies such as helping them communicate clearly to others what they are experiencing with the side effects. This is so that they can let the people around them know when they need time out, when they are feeling overwhelmed, or when they are feeling angry, upset or distressed. Some people find that the most helpful strategy when these hormonal surges are happening is to stay away from others, restricting visits. As long as this is a relatively short-term strategy it can be an effective tool.

### Antinausea Drugs

Unfortunately, several commonly used antinausea drugs can have significant impacts on young people. Most commonly, these side effects are recognisable by their profile and are ceased quickly, for instance, lock jaw with Stemetil tablet use (prochlorperazine). However, some effects are more subtle, including the symptoms of panic attack with the use of metoclopramide. This drug is used with patients who have found chemotherapy difficult and are suffering severe nausea. Some of these patients can begin to exhibit signs of panic, feeling hot, having difficulty staying in their room, feeling they cannot breathe and needing to 'escape'. They are not, however, suffering actual panic attacks but rather experiencing a physical after-effect of the drug regime. If unrecognised, this may result in the young person actually developing secondary anxiety.

It is important to provide a thorough assessment for any young person to identify significant change in presentation, including feeling anxious or having hallucinatory experiences in the context of their use of the above medications. These effects often occur in the context of intramuscular or intravenous use of the drugs, however, similar effects can be seen in oral use for patients who are susceptible to them. Generally, once the drug ceased the symptoms will reduce/ disappear, with the exception of situations such as described above, where the patient develops secondary anxiety. Young people often respond well to reassurance and psycho-education about the drug effects, which can often alleviate some of the secondary anxiety, however, some young people will also require structured interventions around the management of this anxiety.

# Chapter 7

# Building a Therapeutic Relationship

---

'After 5 years, you are just part of the story, just like the rest of the team.'
— 19-year-old male

---

There is no secret that in therapeutic interventions young people engage differently to adults or children. There is also no hiding the fact that it is often harder to engage young people initially in therapy or intervention. Within the cancer setting, this engagement in therapy is particularly important as there is invariably going to be a period during the treatment or its aftermath that the young person is going to have difficulties coping and managing. Within many health services there will not be the option of providing up-front psychological support to all young people, either in the form of a psychologist, or specially trained other professional. In those services where this is an option, however, early engagement and normalisation of the role of psychological support in the context of their cancer journey is a very effective way of building a strong relationship with young people and their families.

The time of a cancer diagnosis is when families and young people feel a blur of activity is happening — they are still reeling from the news and they feel like they are meeting thousands of people and having to make thousands of decisions. Although it seems that it would not be helpful to engage with people at this time — when they are already feeling quite overwhelmed — paradoxically, the opposite is true. Young people will often recall positively the time when the psychologist first came and met them — the start of the relationship. There is very rarely 'psychological stuff' done on this first meeting, instead it is about simply introducing yourself, your role and some general information about what to expect about whatever procedure is next.

This first meeting is often very general, brief and mostly about putting a face to the role of psychologist for the young person. At the end of this meeting, it is about making a plan to see the young person again, and allowing them to have some decision-making about how they would like this to happen. Often young people will be accompanied by their parents or partners in this initial meeting, and it is important to give future options about how they would like to be seen. If the patient suggests that meeting in a chemotherapy suite is a good option, it should be recognised that this space is not very private and they are likely to be accompanied by their parents. If the patient opts to meet in the counselling room, then it is likely to be a more complete conversation without their parents. Intentionally, the initial session is not a good space to ask much about the more intimate details of their worlds, including relationships, sexuality and so forth, as this will generally be in a very public space (for example, the chemotherapy suite or the clinic reception area).

If there are medical and nursing teams that promote the role of the psychologist within the team, this helps considerably with the young person's initial engagement. However, the most important element of good engagement (outside of building the relationship itself) is about how the concept of psychology is introduced, and what this means in the scheme of the young person's treatment. For instance, if it is introduced along the lines of:

> *Hi, my name is _____ and I am the psychologist who*
> *works with young people here at the hospital. My job is*
> *to help people manage through all of this, as most young*
> *people aren't expecting to have to deal with cancer at this*
> *time in their lives. (Mostly, the young person will agree*
> *at this time.) Hopefully, you will manage all of this well,*
> *but I like to get to know people from the start, just in*
> *case there are times where you need extra support, or are*
> *finding it hard to cope.*

Then, it is about setting expectations for how the interactions will occur. There is no point meeting someone at their first treatment, and then not seeing them again until they are finishing treatment or coming back for scans. Relationship-building with this group of patients is a long-term commitment. From my experience, young people generally won't tell you exactly what is going on until at least three meetings in, even if you are asking specific questions about their situation. Sometimes in the cancer setting this is even longer, as young people are often quite conscious about making sure that everyone in the cancer team has a good impression of how they are doing. This need to make a good impression is often driven by equating difficulty in coping with a false assumption that treatment may be stopped.

For this reason, as well as strategies around building engagement it is important to have a plan about how often you are going to review the young person. (It may just mean checking in with them quickly when they are in clinic.) Most young people are happy to let the clinician lead this process, and if it is suggested that you catch up with them each treatment cycle they will generally agree. For some patients, the week after treatment is the most difficult in terms of managing side effects, so it can be helpful to offer to touch base with them over the phone at that time. As a clinician in this space, an acknowledgment of the physical and emotional vulnerability of the young person is paramount, and this may change the nature of the engagement. This is particularly true for situations where the young person is in hospital or physically very unwell.

Once the therapeutic relationship has been built and the sense that the engagement with the psychologist is normal, young people will willingly engage and be present in the therapeutic space. Furthermore, they will often make contact between sessions and seek support in managing both cancer-related and external concerns, such as relationships with peers, partners and parents, as well as strategies about how to approach particular aspects of their future life. During therapy is often one of the only times that young people will feel safe to articulate the fear, anxiety and worry about whether they may die from their cancer. They will usually express how they really feel about treatment, and will seek support around decision-making about that treatment, as well as expressing existential fear and distress. This therapeutic engagement is important for both the young people as well as the therapist, and young people will become quite protective of that space. In addition, they may seek out 'unofficial' guidance about how the people around them can gain support, including parents and partners.

There will, of course, always be some young people who will be reluctant consumers of psychological therapy. Younger patients particularly will be much more suspicious of the role of the therapist and may be less likely to engage. It is worth persevering with those patients who may initially provide monosyllabic answers and look particularly unimpressed to see you. Generally, there will be a 'tipping point' at which time they will become more engaged and appear more visibly connected to the therapist. Ideally, if patients who are less engaged can be seen without their parents they will often start talking more freely. However, it is often these patients who are reluctant to let their parents leave in the first place, by becoming creative about when you can see the patient can be a good strategy to catch them alone. For instance, early in the morning on the ward, or around lunchtime in the chemotherapy suite (which is often when parents will go in search of food).

Over time, it is not uncommon for parents and partners of the young patient to identify that they are also needing support. It is up to the therapist whether they are also happy to see members of the family, or whether they ask another therapist to review various family members. The young person themselves may not know that their parent or partner has sought support. The family will often want to see the same therapist as they feel confident that he or she has a good understanding of what has happened to date. If confidentially is clearly explained to all members involved in the thera-peutic situation then it is reasonable for one therapist to see various members of the family. Seeing the family members in addition to the patient can provide significantly more context to the young person's situation, as well as the way that they and the people around them cope. This information (albeit held within the therapist's mind rather than identified to the young person) can be a good foundation to build on the therapeutic framework that has been established with the young person and their family.

It is important to note that these relationships can have a significant impact on the therapist, as well as the young person and their family. Many therapists will have a long-term involvement with their young patients — through treatment and into survivorship — with patients often bouncing in and out of therapy depending on their circumstances. Generally, if a young person suffers a relapse in their cancer they will re-engage in therapy to help them manage their reactions, as well as any anxiety around the results of medical scans. Over this period, you may see a young adolescent turn into a young adult, or a young adult move into a very different phase of their lives as they get married, travel, finish university and move out of home.

Almost all relationships of this nature with young people will feel difficult for the therapist at times, and within the cancer setting it is no exception, particularly because these relationships can be long-lasting and have periods of heightened intensity. It is imperative that the therapist can manage their own thoughts, emotions and the impact the young people has on them, and be able to identify when they need to take extra steps to look after themselves. This is of paramount importance after particularly intense engagement with a patient or their families, such as at the end-of-life phase, or when a young person has been hospitalised or critically ill for an extended period.

Although it can feel at times like the therapist is the glue holding everything together for the young person, this is almost never the case, and young people and their families have their own support network that they can access. It is important that therapists have strong boundaries to protect themselves from the sheer intensity of this work.

# Chapter 8

# Relationships

The social networks and engagements of adolescents and young adults change frequently during their life. They may be moving from one social group to another, disconnecting from parents, moving out of home and starting intimate relationships. All these things are typically disrupted in some way or another with a cancer diagnosis. For example, developing relationships can become suspended or go backwards. It is important in therapy to attend to these changing dynamics.

### Peer Relationships

Cancer in adolescence or early adulthood is known to significantly disrupt a young person's social connections and engagement with their same-age peers. Just through the process of treatment, a young person will be removed and isolated from their peers and they may miss significant opportunities for connections with peers and normal activities. This is particularly highlighted for younger adolescents who gain most of their social contact from school or extracurricular activities. Their peers are often unable or ill-equipped to attend hospitals or manage the emotional challenges that come from having a peer with cancer.

One of the biggest challenges for young people during treatment is managing to maintain the connections with their peer group, which can be aided significantly by ongoing engagement with social media and facilitating contact with a school environment. For those who are older, these contacts can often be easily maintained as their friends are more independent and organised, allowing them to have more capacity to visit, or provide support. However, older adolescents and young adults may also have a more complex lifestyle and stressors, which may inadvertently result in less availability to support the young person. Either way, very quickly the young person's life of living with cancer will look very different to those around them, and the gap between peers can become pronounced.

For most young people, their peer relationships will be much more important to them than the relationships they have with family, parents and hospital staff — the most easily accessible engagements for the young person while on treatment. Developing communication strategies and skills to help keep them engaged with their peers while on treatment is therefore incredibly important. Without these ongoing relationships, the young person is at risk not only of emotional difficulties during treatment but also for a more difficult transition at the end of treatment. Therapists can often provide conduits for young people and their peers to remain engaged with each other in several ways, including:

- Helping the young person communicate information about their illness and treatment.
- Supporting the young person to initiate communication concerning how their peers may be feeling about their situation.
- Communication skills to facilitate conversations that are not about their cancer, thereby allowing the young person to feel that they can add something else to the conversation. This becomes particularly important for those who are in hospital for long periods and feel that the world outside is moving on without them.

- Engaging the young person in strategies to help facilitate communication — for instance, scheduling social media time, encouraging a close friend to visit the hospital, engaging parents in helping to manage the logistics around having friends come over.
- Providing education to the school/university/workplace regarding how young people can maintain relationships when someone is in hospital and provide skills for the patient's peers to engage with them.
- Advocating for young people in the above settings, or within particular groups.

Although not possible in all health environments, often the most rewarding peer interaction that young people will talk about during their cancer journey is when they meet another young person in a similar situation. These relationships help normalise the young person's experience. They provide significant validation about how they react emotionally to treatment and bad news, as well as their struggles with coping. Ideally, in each treatment centre there would be a matching process for this, however, even with the charities that exist to facilitate these peer-to-peer contacts, young people will rarely take the initiative, particularly while on treatment. As such, serendipitous meetings are far more effective (particularly if they can be arranged!). It is important to keep in mind though that if a young person becomes more unwell, relapses or dies, the person with whom they have formed relationships will be severely affected. They may require significant support in managing both their grief about their friend as well as issues related to their own disease and sense of mortality.

## Intimate Relationships

Relationships for young people are generally intense and filled with unfamiliar emotions and hormones, particularly when in a relationship for the first time. This is further intensified by issues such as the higher school certificate (HSC), university stress or travel. For young people with cancer these things are even more stressful.

The cancer does not normally impact the young person's want or need to engage in relationships, however, at times the treatment may mean young people question whether it is a good idea to have a relationship. This is more evident for those who have a poor prognosis or who have a known limited life expectancy. When relationships are going well for young people this interaction can be a helpful and protective factor in managing their cancer experience. However, if relationships break down or become difficult to manage, they can cause significant emotional changes and difficulties managing treatment.

It is expected, of course, that young people who experience a relationship breakdown will suffer significant emotional change and distress, regardless of their cancer. If however they are not coping well with the existing stress brought on by the cancer, then they are likely to suffer additional psychological distress when dealing with intimate relationships. It is common for relationships to become volatile and end during the cancer treatment process, and for young people to have limited resources to deal with this. For this reason, young people may have emotional responses that appear quite disproportionate to the situation or length of the relationship, or alternatively, may underreport the sense of importance of the relationship while demonstrating change in emotional states.

> 'The cancer is just another part of our relationship. It's been together with my partner longer than I have.'
> — 27-year-old female

For those young people in relationships during treatment, the patient's partner may also seek out support from the treating team, and will often report feeling quite 'invisible' in the management of the illness as the young person manages the information that is communicated. For those who are separated from the process, either due to the young person's choice or other logistical issues, the partners may feel quite isolated and unaware of what is going on, particularly when the situation is changing. In some families, parents may make a conscious choice to ensure that the young person's partner is included in the discussions around what is happening medically; however, other families may behave in the opposite way — everyone except the immediate family is distanced from the situation. Partners can be particularly emotionally vulnerable at times of medical deterioration or when a young person is forced to be in hospital for a long period. Some patients and their partners develop exceptional skills at managing the cancer as part of their relationship. The cancer and its effect on their lives becomes simply another variable that they manage, along with aspects such as friends, family dynamics and educational choices.

Young people who are unwell may make the conscious decision to disengage from the relationships around them to focus on managing the cancer. This can be quite difficult for the people around them, especially if the relationship is a source of support. Young people may provide very logical and rational reasons for making decisions about their relationships, and will commonly seek support about how to negotiate the emotional aspects of such decisions. During treatment, as young people are removed from their peer group and the unlikelihood they will talk about their intimate relationships with parents, this can become an integral part of the work that is done within the therapeutic relationship.

For those who are entering relationships, or wanting to engage in seeking a partner, their cancer can provide significant anxieties about how this will look, and what they will disclose to their potential partner. Some make an active decision to tell the potential partner at a designated time point, for instance after three dates, or before they become intimate (which may present specific challenges). Others will make the decision to be open about their cancer from the beginning and prevent any worries about people not accepting their cancer and inadvertently, themselves. Uncertainty can be hard to manage in the context of a new relationship, particularly when the young person is feeling vulnerable. Helping to support the young person in developing a sense of how they connect with another person, while they acknowledge their cancer, can help the overall anxiety about building relationships.

## Support strategies for young people in relationships

*Open communication with the young person about what they are sharing with their partner, or potential partner about the cancer.*

Even adults who have had extensive experience in living with cancer find it difficult to talk about their cancer to those around them. It is therefore particularly difficult in the case of young cancer patients, where it is unlikely that the people around them will really understand what it means for a young person to be living with cancer. They can experience significant anxiety about how they communicate about their cancer when attempting to enter a new relationship. They may worry about whether anyone would willingly enter a relationship with someone who is unwell, or if so, what is their motivation for doing so. Similarly, for those who are in relationships, they may make conscious decisions about not talking about their cancer with their partner. Although this can be a helpful protective factor to allow the young person to have a 'cancer-free space' it does, of course, become fraught with danger when it comes to the reality of managing the diagnosis and treatment. Sometimes gentle psycho-education and prompting can help a young person explore their anxieties and worries about discussing their cancer with their partner and how they manage this.

### Support in decision-making.

Working with the young person to make decisions about how they engage with relationships may include problem-solving any potential outcomes and implications of ending relationships, as well as the impact of starting or staying in a relationship. For instance, if a young person is wanting to end the relationship and their partner is the main support, you will need to prepare them for the reality that this person may be unable to support them anymore and to then explore how they will cope with that, as well as other avenues of support that they will need to establish.

### Psycho-education and guidance around external factors which may impact behaviours or decisions in the relationship.

At many times during the cancer process young people may feel very much out of control and will grasp aspects of their lives they feel they control. For instance, for young people who are recovering posttreatment and adjusting to permanent impairment in functioning, their tolerance for changes in a partner's behaviours or otherwise may evoke much stronger responses emotionally than in the past. If young people can have a context around managing these changes, such as delaying significant decision-making or ensuring that they have a good understanding of the impact of their decisions, it can allow them a greater sense of control, even if they ultimately decide not to make changes at that time.

### Manage fallout.

Even for young people who are convinced about their decision-making in relationships, including ending or telling a new partner about the cancer, the other person's reaction can be highly variable. In addition, the young person can experience significant emotional responses that they may not have been expecting. It is important that there remains a safe space for them to be able to process the impact of these emotions, as well as any existential distress that comes from such.

Although not the focus of this chapter, it is imperative to note the impact of cancer and its treatments on sexual intimacy, as well as body image overall. For most young people, the time of their cancer will coincide with the height of sexual experimentation and identify formation. For those who are in sexual relationships or sexually active, treatments can have a significant impact on both psychological and physiological factors related to sensation, drive, enjoyment and function. Although many of these factors are temporary and will be corrected by completion of treatment, young people will still undergo adjustment and grief around changes to their function and engagement in sexual activities.

For those who have not engaged in sexual activities previously, the anxiety around their function and ability may be overwhelming. They may find that they are unable to progress within relationships. Although the focus of our discussions here are not medical, many concerns of young people around sexuality can be managed easily with open and frank discussions around their sexual function and emotions associated with such. The challenge for many professionals can be related to their own embarrassment about raising concerns about sexuality; however, young people are generally relieved when health professionals initiate discussion and information-giving about sexual function.

It is worth mentioning here the impact of body image changes on intimacy and relationships. (See chapter 11 for a full discussion about body image.) Changes to their body image because of treatment are likely to have a significant impact on young people's relationships and intimacy. Often, these may be temporary, such as hair loss or weight gain, and young people may find that when these concerns resolve their difficulties will also resolve. However, there may be other more permanent or challenging body image concerns for young people, such as those who have function-impairing surgery, formation of stomas, amputations or cognitive impairments. Young people are likely to need specific interventions and support in adjusting to the change in their body image and the ways in which they can work with these changes in the context of their relationships to others, as well as a sense of self.

## Relationship to parents

There have been volumes written about the impact of cancer on young people's relationship to their parents. Depending on the age at diagnosis, as well as the relationship that exists between parents and child, the change in the relationship may be highly significant or only mildly changed. For instance, the young person who is in their early adolescence still living at home will adapt differently to the young person who is forced to move back home following diagnosis for their parent/s to be their primary caregivers.

Following diagnosis, challenges exist in the relationship for both the parents and young people that become evident in the ongoing nature of the treatment process — with roles and identity having significant shifts. Young people readily identify the support from their parents as paramount and unquestionable; however, they can also articulate the struggle in managing their interactions with their parents. Again, this can be more pronounced in those who have been out of home for some time, or had been living independently from their parents prior to diagnosis. This may result in young people 'reverting' back to adolescent behaviour and finding that both they and their parents will revisit periods of earlier conflict. This is more pronounced when there are additional stressors to the cancer, such as the HSC or other expectation-based components. It is at this time that parents may attribute significant importance to things that may not be shared by the young person. This has the potential to cause conflict around how they manage workload and other activities.

> 'They just keep going on about getting good marks in the HSC. It's just the HSC. After having chemo, the HSC will be easy to manage.'
> — 17-year-old female

The needs of parents can easily be overlooked within the healthcare setting, with young people generally the focus not only of interventions, but also support. It is important that parents are also able to have space around managing their emotions (which is not shared with their children) as well as group sessions when needed for young people and their parents to speak in a moderated space around differing needs and points of conflict. It is also helpful to have open conversations and discussions with both young people and their families about the role of their relationship and how this may change over time. By allowing these conversations to develop, young people can build a context for the emotional challenges their parents face in managing their treatment, and parents gain an understanding of the normal emotional responses of young people during and after the treatment process.

# Chapter 9

# Fertility and Sexuality

Fertility and conception are things that most young people have not considered in any meaningful way prior to a cancer diagnosis. For most, they may have had fleeting thoughts about whether they might want to have children in the future, or perhaps decided that this is something they don't want. Some young people may have partners. Rarely have these relationships been longstanding or ones in which the issues about potentially parenting children together in the future have been addressed.

The issues around fertility preservation for young people has become increasingly emphasised over the past decade and identified as a significant implication of treatment that will continue to have an impact for the rest of the young person's life. Most hospitals that offer treatment to young people will have protocols around the management of fertility preservation and the ongoing management of treatment induced fertility concerns. Almost all young people will be given the option to preserve their fertility, the exception being those who are too unwell, or who need to start treatment immediately due to the life-threatening nature of their disease.

For males at diagnosis, the steps for fertility preservation are relatively easy, in theory. Any young male who is at risk of losing his fertility through chemotherapy will be given the option of sperm banking prior to starting treatment. For most young men, this is non-invasive and easily managed, if not a bit awkward. However, for those young people who are on high doses of pain medication or who are unwell, they may be physiologically unable to proceed with sperm collection, and may require more invasive collection techniques should they choose to go ahead. The decision-making process for young men is generally straightforward following this point — should they have their fertility be maintained following treatment then they can opt to have their samples destroyed, and if not, they can store them and use them as needed in the future.

Female fertility preservation is a more complex situation that is more invasive for the patient. Young women can experience significant impacts of treatment including entering a temporary or permanent menopause. Initially, young women need to make the decision about even proceeding with preservation, or whether they should opt to start cancer treatment right away. Unlike young men who can complete sperm banking in a couple of days, a cycle to harvest eggs can take several weeks depending on where the patient is in her menstrual cycle. In some situations, this is simply not a medical option. Furthermore, success is maximised for those who can store fertilised eggs (embryos) rather than unfertilised eggs, which can lead to quite complex discussions and decision-making around whether the patient's current partner is an appropriate person with whom to create embryos. As imagined, in the context of situations where a relationship is relatively new, or casual, the impact of these discussions can be a huge strain in addition to the cancer diagnosis itself. Young women are also more likely to experience hormonal effects from cancer treatments and may experience premature menopause.

For some, there is not even time to make a choice about fertility preservation. For these young people, the immediacy of the event means they are unable to make some sort of rational decision about how they will deal with this in their future life. Those young people who choose to opt out of fertility preservation, for any number of reasons, the uncertainty around their fertility status can be much more difficult to manage. They can find the completion of treatment nerve-racking as they wait to assess what has happened to their reproductive function. When young people are making decisions to not attempt preservation, it is important that they are given all the appropriate information about what this decision means for their future, as well as the likelihood of other fertility issues arising posttreatment, such as menopause. Ideally, all young patients should be given the opportunity to discuss their decision-making with a fertility specialist prior to beginning treatment, when medically appropriate.

An issue predominately for women, but which can affect all young people, is the impact of treatment on sexual function. This may be due to hormonal changes, such as menopause, or decimation of testosterone, but may also be around difficulties with regulating hormones, or being able to perform sexually due to neuropathy, or changes in nerve function. Young people will often need specialist intervention in this case — both medically and psychologically. This can be particularly troublesome for young women who may lose both sensation and lubrication in their vagina following treatment. This can have considerable psychological consequences for not only sense of self, but also engagement with potential partners, and their sense of future.

# Chapter 10

# Drugs and Alcohol

Drug and alcohol use unfortunately form a significant part of youth culture and peer group engagement. Those who are living with cancer are not exempt from this. There can often be a 'catch-up' period at the end of treatment where they may use these substances more heavily than their peers who have been able to moderate their use.

Generally, young people are not feeling well enough during treatment to consider engaging in alcohol and drug use. While some may be able to tolerate drinking while on chemotherapy or radiotherapy, most will report feeling very unwell following any substance use and this is enough to encourage them to abstain through treatment. At the end of treatment, however, several things can accumulate for young people that may lead to them re-engaging with alcohol. Firstly, they will have missed many engagements and social processes because of their treatment. This can mean that young people will 're-emerge' into their social scene and feel compelled to catch up for lost time, which may include partying much harder than they would have previously. Secondly, finishing treatment is known to have emotional ramifications that are significant in terms of how young people relate to the world, as well as to their own sense of self and purpose. Young people may speak about the use of drugs and alcohol as a buffer for managing these emotions, and of feeling unencumbered by them through such use. Finally, surviving cancer can further perpetuate a young person's innate sense of invincibility that can drive increased generalised risk taking. This is often fuelled by feeling that 'nothing worse than cancer' can happen to them.

Occasionally, the impact of the diagnosis and treatment will have the opposite effect on young people such that they abstain from substances readily used prior to diagnosis. While this decision can also be multifactorial, it is often based on a sense that the young person considers they had been making poor choices prior to their diagnosis, and has now made a conscious decision to make better choices following treatment. This can also reflect the young person's heightened awareness about their body, and the way that they engage with their health. They may make decisions to change behaviours for the better, such as increasing exercise, changing their diet, improving work/study habits, as well as changing drug and alcohol intake.

To assess a young person's drug and alcohol habits, it is best to be frank and transparent from the beginning (this approach also applies to asking difficult questions about sexuality, sexual behaviours and other risk taking). Generally, if asked in an appropriate context, young people will happily engage in discussions about their drug and alcohol use (if any), as well as how the other people around them engage in these behaviours. They will also be able to provide information about how they feel about the use of these things, and whether they feel that they will be a problem for them. A good lead-in to asking about these behaviours is to use questions about how they engage with their friends, for instance 'what do you and your friends get up to?' or 'are you and your friends going out much?' Depending on their answers to these questions, it's easy to segue into further exploration of their own habits and behaviours. Young people can be surprisingly open about their use of substances, and providing you as the therapist are able to engage well with them around these issues, they are unlikely to be reluctant to work with you regarding any issues that may arise.

When providing psycho-education about drug and alcohol use, it can be helpful to give context rather than information. In the case of marijuana use for nausea, for example, young people will respond much more favourably to an open discussion about what other young people have experienced. For instance, 'many of my young patients have tried using it to manage their nausea and symptoms, and it can go either way. For some people it is really helpful, but for others it makes them feel worse'. Alternatively, 'it may help with the nausea, but many of the young people I see find the anxiety they get afterwards really hard to manage'. Chances are, if a young person is asking you about it, they are already using the substance, or seriously considering it. For this reason, simply telling them not to do it is likely to not only alienate the young person, but may also be rather unhelpful. By focusing on a harm minimisation approach, rather than abstinence, it is a much more therapeutically productive process and also allows more frank discussion in the future around the management of their uses. This discussion can become particularly important in the case of long hospitalisations (if a patient has become a regular user of substances to manage symptoms or anxiety) as well as at end of life, when patients may be reluctant to disclose use. This can have significant impacts on efficacy and effects of medications used for symptom management.

Throughout treatment, young people may also be exposed to other drugs that can become drugs of dependency or habit forming. Although it is unlikely that these will cause significant problems for most patients who use them, there are some young people who will use them inappropriately for management of anxiety or low mood. For all patients, it is imperative that the psychotropic symptoms of medications are monitored, including reducing efficacy of benzodiazepines (such as Lorazepam – commonly used in chemotherapy and for the management of anticipatory anxiety) or pain killers, which may be an indicator of increasing use. Young people respond well to education about the reasons why these medications are limited, and are generally open to suggestions around managing the underlying problems, rather than having to take medication. For those who are using them inappropriately, they will need close evaluation and monitoring, particularly if there is a risk of withdrawal or rebound anxiety/depression on completion of a medication, which may be best managed by a specialist psychiatrist or drug and alcohol team.

# Chapter 11

# Body Image

---

'How am I meant to have sex with this thing [referring to stoma]? I
don't want to look at it, how could anyone else be ok with it?'
— 22-year-old woman

---

Unfortunately, as a result of treatment many young people
will be left with challenging, and sometimes permanent
changes to their bodies and perceptions of their self-image.
As touched on in earlier chapters, such changes mean that
young people may have significant impacts on their level of
function (for instance, an amputation, hormonal changes
or stoma bag) as well as cosmetic changes (skin pigmenta-
tion, hair loss and scarring). Many young people will adapt
over time to these changes, integrate these 'new elements' of
themselves into their self-perception and develop strategies
to explain these changes to other people. For some, however,
these changes can lead to significant psychological distress
and impairment in interpersonal relationships.

> *Jane is a 18-year-old woman who required a forequarter
> amputation (nondominant hand) for the management
> of an osteosarcoma. Although she understood that the
> surgery would result in the loss of her arm, it was not until
> after the surgery that she was able to conceptualise what
> the reality of missing one arm meant. From frustrations
> about not being able to wear the clothing that she likes
> (unable to do up buttons, shoelaces or belts) she reports*

*that she hates the look of herself, and 'feels sick' whenever*
*she looks at her stump/missing arm. Jane reports that she*
*has significant phantom limb pain that has not improved*
*with medications, and feels that she can't live like this with*
*'everyone staring' at her 'all the time'.*

Jane's situation is not uncommon, with the abstract sense
of the outcome of an intervention being quite different to
the day-to-day reality of living with a stoma, amputation or
other body-altering process. For all young people undergoing
these transitions, there is a period of adjustment and is quite
common immediately following surgeries that young people
may actively avoid engaging in the care of their wound,
stomas or scars. This is particularly the case when young
people require either a colostomy or ileal conduit. By their
very nature, these surgeries and the development of these
stomas are confronting, and have far-reaching consequences
for the young person's functional change and also around
sexuality, sexual function and external sense of self.

'Can you believe it, he asked to see my stoma bag? I haven't
asked him to show me his bum.'
— 18-year-old male.

It is a huge transition and adjustment for a young person to
make sense of these changes for themselves; however, this is
complicated significantly by the engagement in others around
these changes. It is not uncommon for others to either speak
open and frankly about the changes, or to become fixated on
the change. For instance, a young person's family member
who constantly asks about their surgery/scar progress and
asks to see such, without realising the impact of the young
person. Alternatively, young people will express a sense that
people disconnect from them for fear of the change and want
to avoid talking about it. This is particularly problematic for

younger adolescents who return to school posttreatment with obvious physical changes and who find that their peer group do not engage with them in the same way. In the context of the rest of the changes associated with the cancer, this may result in young people feeling isolated, and at high risk for poor re-engagement into their 'normal life' posttreatment.

Even for the temporary side effects, such as hair loss or skin changes, the difficulty for young people to manage these cannot be underestimated. Within the seriousness of the disease, these changes can often be downplayed or minimised as a simple 'cost' of the treatment, which will return to normal when everything is completed. Young people who have strong relationships/connections to their changing body image may require significant support in managing both the anticipation and reality of what life on treatment will mean. For both young men and women, the anticipation of losing their hair, however temporary, is distressing and not simply about the hair itself. It also encapsulates worries about identity, a public perception of being unwell, and a sense of discomfort about what it means to have no hair. Some can move through this once their hair actually falls out, finding the anticipation worse than the reality. However, some can become paralysed by the loss of hair, including social withdrawal until treatment stops and hair starts to grow back (which may take several months).

> 'Having my leg cut off wasn't me being brave. It was just what had to be done.'
> — 23-year-old male

When working with young people with body image concerns, the most important aspect of engagement is around allowing them to acknowledge the distress they are experiencing. Many young people will speak about the pressure on them to just 'be ok' with the changes, and find that the space they can have with the therapist may be the only time when they can truly be honest about how they feel. The reality for many of the young people is that these changes are confronting to everyone around them, even to you as a therapist. For instance, it may be quite hard to sit with a patient who has a significant facial disfigurement, or a malodourous tumour. Young people living with these concerns are acutely aware of their impact and, as such, it is often worth exploring these feelings and allowing them to explore how it feels to have people 'staring' at them, or perhaps what is even more difficult to manage, when people are 'looking away'. Patients will often get to a point where they can reconcile these difficulties for themselves, and will report not noticing other' reactions anymore; but getting to this point (if ever) takes a significant amount of adjustment and support.

There is a challenge for those who are living with permanent body image changes regarding how they then build a relationship to the changes, and how they begin to manage the impact of the change. Some of these changes may become easier to manage over time, however, in the initial stages there will be situations occurring on a daily/weekly basis requiring the young person to build effective strategies. This is particularly the case with those who have experienced functional change, and who need to relearn how to do even very simple things, often resulting in high levels of frustration and intolerance. Working within an ACT framework can often be helpful for managing the young person's own thoughts about their body image as well as helping to provide a context for thoughts of hopelessness about their future, and the ways that others interact with them. In the first instance, this may be quite challenging for the young person, and for the therapist the first couple of months' postsurgery/interventions may actually feel more like a debriefing/containment session rather than a strategy-based intervention. As the young person moves through their own grief and frustrations it will allow further space to explore these relationships and cognitive processes.

# Chapter 12

# Managing Depression in the Cancer Context

Just as they experience anxiety, it is not unexpected that some of the young people who undergo treatment for cancer will have difficulties with depression. Their cancer treatment can become overwhelming and unrelenting. Young people are ultimately taken away from their normal lives for a prolonged period, and may experience significant changes in perception related to the meaning of their existence. All these factors, as well as having periods of being unwell, can perpetuate periods of low mood. In my experience, it is less likely that a young person will experience a major depressive episode in the context of treatment than experiencing significant anxiety; however, in the survivorship period depressive symptoms are more common. It is important to discern between the differences in transient mood changes because of the cancer or its treatment as compared to a major depressive episode, particularly within the context of an active treatment environment. One of the most obvious and easiest screens that can detect depression in young people simply involves asking them if they feel depressed. This can provide a very telling response, with young people who are experiencing treatment-related difficulties generally able to articulate that when treatment is completed, or on their 'good chemo weeks', they will feel better. Below is a table of the common symptoms of low mood and treatment effects and ways of discerning the difference between normal adjustment and depression.

**Table 12.1**

| Symptom | Context in which it is commonly seen | Normal Adjustment or Depressive Episode |
|---|---|---|
| Low Motivation | During chemotherapy or radiotherapy Prolonged hospital admissions Recovery from treatment Following weight gain Brain involvement from disease | Can be both, however is generally related to treatment. If the low motivation continues when the young person is recovered and well, it is more likely to be related to depressive symptoms |
| Withdrawal | During chemotherapy or radiotherapy Prolonged hospital admissions During the survivorship period | Can be both, however periods of withdrawal is very common for young people who have prolonged admissions or complex physical concerns. This is generally transient, and although they may withdraw from staff and parents at this time, when questioned they may continue to engage in social media, even though they might not be actively contributing. Again, if this continues at the completion of treatment when they are well, it can be a sign of mood disturbance. |

| Irritability | During chemotherapy or radiotherapy Prolonged hospital admissions Effects of Steroids | Very common, particularly for young men during treatment, particularly in the context of steroids (including ceasing steroids). Irritability tends to increase as the treatment period increases or in the context of pain. |
| --- | --- | --- |
| Thoughts of self-harm or suicidal ideation | During chemotherapy or radiotherapy Prolonged hospital admissions In the context of ongoing unmanaged symptoms, particularly pain Relapse of disease/ Poor Prognosis | These symptoms are much more likely to be representational of a depressive episode than of treatment effects. That said however, for some patients who have particularly hard to manage pain, difficult disease, or uncertain prognosis can express ideas around suicidal ideation as a mechanism of voicing frustration and sense of helplessness. |
| Racing Thoughts/ Ruminating Worries | Steroid effects Other medication effects | Steroids provide significant impairment for cognitive processes, including racing thoughts and at times ruminations. If these ruminations or racing thoughts are happening when the young person has been off steroids for a period of time it is more likely to be anxiety/low mood related. |

| Sleep and Appetite Changes | During chemotherapy or radiotherapy Prolonged hospital admissions Steroid effects | These symptoms in themselves are not helpful markers, as almost all young people who have treatment will experience sleep and appetite disturbance at some time. However, if this remains pervasive at the completion of treatment or if the young person has had significant problems managing either of these factors in the past it is a cause for concern. |
|---|---|---|
| Sense of helplessness/ hopelessness | During chemotherapy or radiotherapy In the context of ongoing unmanaged symptoms, particularly pain Prolonged hospital admissions At relapse/End of Life | In the context of particular aspects of treatment feelings of helplessness are quite common, particularly when things are going poorly with treatment or disease progression. Thoughts of hopelessness are much less common and a more reliable indicator of depression in a young person. The exception to this may be around end of life, when the young person's sense of hopelessness may well be justified. |

There are, of course, many situations where it becomes very hard to separate these symptoms of normal adjustment from depression in the context of difficult treatments.

Regardless of the mechanism driving some of the above symptoms, however, behavioural activation methods such as activity, pleasure and achievement scheduling will generally result in an improvement. Often for these patients just the process of getting up and moving around can have really significant impacts on mood and motivation, even when physically unwell. This is particularly the case for those who are in hospital for prolonged periods, or have rigorous and demanding chemotherapy schedules. When providing activity scheduling activities while someone is unwell, it is even more important that the activities be very small and achievable, as their tolerance will generally be less than found even in a very depressed person as their physical capacity is much lower. This is particularly true when exploring how to manage exercise engagement or energy-dense activities, such as having peers visiting. Many young people will have a good sense of what they can manage given their physical state, and will work easily around this. Table 12.2 provides an example of an activity schedule for a young person in hospital for a long admission. Within a hospital, activity schedules may need to be flexible and consider the young person's physical activity levels, preference for activities and ability to leave the ward. These can also be used easily for young people once they have gotten out of hospital and can form the basis of a gradual recovery program. It is important to emphasise to the young person that the activities related to pleasure and achievement are the priorities for them, as the hospital tends to remove much sense of this for most patients.

**Table 12.2**

| Time | Activity |
|---|---|
| 6:30 – 7:30 | Lay in bed and hope that the nurses let me sleep in! |
| 7:30 – 8am | Breakfast and medications |
| 8am – 10am | Shower, doctors rounds etc. |
| 10am – 10:15 | Do 3 laps of the corridor from the nurses station to the front door |
| 10:15 – 10:30 | Rest |
| 10:30 – 11:30 | Watch episode of favourite show |
| 11:30 – 12:30 | Do 1 Sudoku puzzle (2 if I get time) |
| 12-30 – 1:30 | Lunch and meds |
| 1:30 – 1:45 | Do 3 laps of the corridor from the nurses station to the front door |
| 1:45 – 3:00 | Rest, or watch some TV if not sleepy! |
| 3:00 – 4:00 | Read 3 chapters of book (if attention span is feeling ok!) |
| 4:00 – 5:30 | Log onto Social Media and connect with friends |
| 5:30 – 6:30 | Dinner and meds |
| 6:30 – 9:30 | Visit by Family |
| 9:30 – 10 | Shower |
| 10:30 - | Sleep! |

Those patients who are experiencing more significant symptoms consistent with depression are managed in a similar way to conventional treatment. However, for the young person with cancer, particularly those having active treatment, the complexities associated with managing factors such as motivation and engagement may not be accurate markers of their improvement. In those who have worries and thoughts related to their illnesses, often the strategies outlined in the anxiety section (see chapter 19) will be useful as young people focus on working out ways to manage their thoughts and worries about a potentially realistic situation. This is very much the case for those who are fearful of treatment-related symptoms, or who form ruminations about pain and their coping skills, as these thoughts are likely to represent very real and terrifying scenarios for the patient. As such, working with strategies that allow them to recognise these thoughts and develop strategies to manage them is more effective than working on ways of challenging or denying the thoughts, to only have the symptoms that they are fearful of appear later.

# Chapter 13

# Risk Assessment and Self-Harm

In the context of a life-threatening illness it is not unexpected that young people would consider ending their lives. This is particularly so when coupled with invasive treatment, symptoms and uncertainty. For many young people they will be reluctant to discuss these thoughts, as they are fearful of the impact of these conversations on their family and care team. Even in this context, however, young people who are expressing suicidal ideation and self-harming behaviours are at high risk, and need to be assessed and managed as such. For young people who are impulsive and have access to means to cause self-harm (which patients often will including pain and other medications) thorough risk assessment and management plans need to be implemented. These will generally require input from others in the young person's care team and their parents (or support person).

> *Katie is a 23-year-old woman who has recently completed treatment for acute leukaemia. She had a history of depression and self-harm prior to her diagnosis, and has shown symptoms of depression throughout her treatment, which have been managed. She indicates that she is convinced that her disease will recur, and reports ruminating and intrusive thoughts about this that she feels unable to manage at times. She indicates in session that she has started self-harming again, which has mainly been superficial-level cutting on her arms and legs, but has also been picking at her incision site for a recently removed Hickman's line. She*

*denies any specific wish to die, but indicates that if her leukaemia were to come back, she would kill herself immediately. She would not tell you about the specifics of this, but alluded to access to significant amounts of narcotics (both prescription and street). You know from attending the multidisciplinary meetings that she has quite high-risk disease, and has a high chance of relapse.*

For most clinicians, Katie's case would cause sleepless nights. She is a good example of a young person who has a history which, in itself, would be causing concern, coupled with high-risk disease, access to means and a re-engagement in self-harming behaviour. Katie has spoken openly about her plans to kill herself if she were to relapse, and has access to means that have the potential to be fatal. When working with a young person who is self-harming, in some ways the interventions are the same as those who do not have a cancer diagnosis. For most young people within the 'cancer system' there is access to several teams and healthcare professionals who can add additional support, including psychiatry and their treating physician. Often, through many months of treatments and procedures, the young person and their family will perceive the hospital team as a 'safe place' and are more likely to raise concerns with these professionals than those in the community from whom they may feel distanced.

In Katie's situation, it would be paramount to engage her in strategies to help manage the self-harming behaviour, and to provide a safe space for her to talk about her concerns about the relapse and what is driving the self-harming behaviour. In addition, she is likely to have very poor tolerance of any change in her physical symptoms (as this may herald the return of her cancer) and as a result may become more unstable in her mood and self-harming behaviours. For young people who have had longstanding self-harming behaviours, at times of high stress (including the completion of treatment), they may be particularly difficult for them to manage, particularly if their driver for the behaviour is related to control.

> 'I said I would kill myself if another person asked me to give blood. No one asked any more questions, and before I knew it I had a psychiatrist at the end of my bed'
> — 19-year-old male

In regard to managing risk and safety it is important that young people have the space to feel heard, particularly in the context of disease. It is not uncommon for young people to speak about opting out of treatment, or not being able to conceptualise what it would be like to have to live through more treatment. This becomes particularly evident in patients who are distressed, or frustrated but when asked further about any ideas around this, they often will indicate that they do not have any plan that they would ever engage in these behaviours. By normalising the reasoning for why young people may find themselves having these thoughts or behaviours, it is often helpful to give them context. For example:

> Your brain has a job. It solves problems. Right now, to solve the problem of you being uncomfortable and in pain, one of the solutions would be to not be here anymore. That idea doesn't have to happen, it's about your brain trying to help you. You can come up with other solutions as well. Most patients in your situation would have these thoughts some time, and that's ok, we just need to work out a way for you to manage them.

By framing the thoughts in this way, it allows the young person to have some space to be able to work with them and separate the utility of the thought from the overwhelming worry and fear about the content of the thought. You can then work with the young person in identifying strategies that can help manage the thoughts, when they might appear, and provide assurance that they do not have any intention of doing anything to act on the thoughts.

In the case of Katie, however, who has paired these concerns with an intention to end her life rather than suffering through further treatment, there is a more sinister risk. For Katie, it would be appropriate to have an open and frank discussion about the impact that the thoughts are having and exploring the reasons behind her fear. For instance, is she making a decision that she would kill herself because she is worried about the pain that she would experience around relapse, or does she see this as a way to avoid further treatment? Dependant on the answers to these things, the way that the situation would be approached could be very different. If Katie had indicated that she is anxious and fearful of pain, then there are many ways to work with her and reassure her around end of life pain management. Or, conversely, if she indicated that she did not want to have further treatment, but knows that all of the people around her would push her to do so, interventions could be implemented around how she communicates this information, and providing her with support in decision-making. When working with young people around relapse and declining treatment they will often report a sense from those around them that they need to 'do everything' to manage the disease, even if they feel that there is a futility in doing so. This can be a driver for thoughts around suicide and self-harm as it allows a reconnection with an ability to control their surroundings and decision-making.

A safety plan and comprehensive ongoing risk assessment would be appropriate when working with Katie, and it is advisable to engage a further person to also review the patient (this is particularly important if they have been known to you for a long time). When a clinician has known a patient for a long time, they can find themselves getting 'stuck', as well as being particularly aware of the relationship between patient and therapist that may cloud interventions and reactions to particular situations. This becomes even more important in the context of managing thoughts and risk of self-harm, as a new provider can provide a 'new' view of the situation and can often provide insights into how to manage such.

# Chapter 14

# Decision-making

---

'If my cancer comes back, I am not having any treatment.'
— Every young person at the completion of chemotherapy

---

There are many assumptions that accompany young people's decision-making. First and foremost, and consciously or not, most people around the young person — including their parents, health professionals and wider community — will assume that when given a diagnosis, or news of progression/relapse, young people will actively engage in treatment. Second, there is often an unspoken and pervasive cultural norm that suggests young people will keep 'fighting' their cancer until the very end, without any question. Of course, there are young people who will fit into both of these categories, however, there are just as many young people who do not. The purpose of this chapter is not to direct a dialogue that forces young people to have treatment, or strategies to ensure that they do not question what is happening medically. Instead, it is about helping to empower young people to manage their situation and make informed choices about what happens to them. For the current chapter, it is assumed that most young people discussed here are over 18, as the process for young people under this age opting out of treatment is more complex and is discussed in detail in the next chapter on competency.

'It all just happened so fast. Before I knew it, I was having chemo. I have realised later, that I never really understood what that would mean, or whether I even wanted it in the first place.'
— 23-year-old

Very commonly, young people will speak about the sense of feeling that they didn't have a choice when it comes to treatment. Partially, they will articulate this around knowing that without treatment for their cancer, they will ultimately die, thus treatment feels like a more reasonable option. This, of course, is a very powerful motivator for most young people and represents a way to survive their cancer and return to a version of their life before cancer. However, discussion around the lack of 'choice' they feel that they have may arise during treatment or later, when they have had time to process the impact and implications of what treatment really looks like, and how their lives are different. In the context of long chemotherapy protocols, young people may question the value and reasons for continuing in the face of what can be overwhelming feelings of hopelessness, as well as insurmountable side effects. Similarly, for a patient who has a function-changing surgery, such as an amputation or permanent colostomy bag, they may question the meaning of life following these events, and ultimately the cost of surviving cancer. Although young people will generally adjust to all aspects mentioned above, for some the space to be able share their worries about treatment, as well as their frustrations of their situation can allow them to make better sense of why they are continuing with treatment. It is very reasonable to question these things, particularly when the intervention may be perceived as worse than the disease (often seen in those patients who were asymptomatic, or had few symptoms from their cancers prior to diagnosis).

Young people have the option to opt out of treatment. Most patients will contemplate this at some time during their treatment; however, in the early stages of disease almost none will go through with this decision. It is important not to pathologise this, instead working with the young person to navigate through the difficult feelings which will arise as a result. More often, discussions and declarations about wanting to stop treatment are more related to being frustrated and 'over' the process rather than wanting to actually stop treatment. When speaking to young people about these issues, they can often clearly articulate that they know that stopping treatment will ultimately impact their prognosis, and do not want to die from their cancer. Being able to normalise this for the young person generally resolves most of their concern and simply being able to give them context for how other young people have coped with similar situations can often alleviate the distress being caused by the frustration and situation.

The most distressing situations where young people opt to not have treatment is when they present with early-stage, or potentially very curable disease. Within the medical community decisions such as these are not seen to make sense, and the health professionals presented with this problem can become very overwhelmed and distressed by working with the young person and their family around their decision to not have treatment. There can be many and varied reasons for why someone might refuse treatment, but the most common are generally related to specific religious and cultural beliefs around cancer and its treatment, or decisions to seek non pharmaceutical-based regimes. For both these reasons, there are arguments for and against the legitimacy and rationale for a young person opting to refuse treatment, but ultimately if the young person is seen to be competent to make decisions around this, they can make the decision to not have treatment.

For those who do decide that they want to stop treatment, it is of paramount importance that they are not making this decision based on either internal (depression, anxiety, medical issues) or external (parents, friends, media) factors that may be clouding their judgement. The issues around competency will be explored further in the following chapter, however, if there is any doubt around a young person's ability to make a decision preventing them having potentially life-saving treatment they require significant assessment by specialist staff to ensure their competence. If a young person (over the age of 18) is competent and feels they want to make the decision to stop treatment, they are able to do so.

> Kip is a 23-year-old who has recently been told that he has relapsed from Ewing's sarcoma. Kip has been seeing the psychologist regularly as he has been convinced that he was going to relapse, and had been feeling very depressed and questioning the purpose of living in this context. From the time that Kip had completed his initial chemotherapy and surgery, he had been adamant that he would not have further treatment if his cancer returned, and knew that he would die relatively quickly as a result. He is asymptomatic of his cancer, and has agreed that he would have some noninvasive treatment if he got symptoms, but is focused on engaging with palliative care and enjoying the time that he has left.

There are very few pleasant aspects about treatment for cancer and it is hardly surprising that young people will attest strongly that they will not have further treatment if their cancer returns. There is a reality, however, that for almost all these patients, if their cancer returns they will have treatment. Hopefully, a significant period of time has passed for them between completing treatment and restarting it, and the memories of their difficulties with treatment may have faded somewhat. However, more importantly, an inbuilt survival instinct kicks in and the young person and their family will quickly re-enter 'action mode', and get back into the treatment habits. This is not to understate the impact that restarting treatment will have psychologically, but generally, young people are able to manage the return to the treatment/ hospital roundabout.

For those who do opt to refuse treatment on the return of their cancer, their decision can have widespread implications for them, their families and also the treatment teams who can find these decisions very difficult to manage. Many young people who make this decision can usually present very logical arguments as to why they do not want to go through with further treatment, not the least of which is often a sense that they know their chance of survival is lower than previously, and question the merit of doing further treatment that is likely to make them unwell and that they may perceive as futile. Young people don't contemplate these decisions lightly, and as such it is important to not brush off these concerns when they are presented, even if for the clinician these may raise challenges to your own ideas.

Working with the young person around their reasons for wanting to stop treatment can be a helpful tool to open dialogue around the implications of what stopping or refusing treatment might look like for them. Examples of some of these questions are listed overleaf.

**Table 14.1**

| Question | Exploration questions and themes |
|---|---|
| Do you have particular reasons for wanting to stop treatment? | 1. If they identify side effects as the main reasons, then it is about exploring whether those side effects can be better managed, or eliminated. And if so, would the treatment feel manageable enough to continue?<br><br>2. Are there peer or social factors which are influencing their decision?<br><br>3. Are they fearful of the treatment itself? (Most common in those who refuse initial treatment). What can be done to manage that fear?<br><br>4. Is their quality of life significantly impacted by their treatment?<br><br>5. Do they have mood or anxiety symptoms which are impacting their ability to make a rational decision around this? |
| What would happen if you stopped treatment? | 1. Do they have a realistic understanding of what will happen if they stop treatment? For instance, can they articulate the symptoms of the cancer are likely to get worse and they will die from the cancer (eventually), or do they think that it will all be ok?<br><br>2. Do they have realistic expectations about what it will look like if they have treatment stop? Do they have expectations that life will simply return to 'normal' as it was pre cancer?<br><br>3. If they can articulate that they will die, do they have an understanding of this. This is particularly important in young people who are emotionally immature, or those who have limited understanding of consequences. |

| Question | Exploration questions and themes |
|---|---|
| If you stop treatment, would you feel ok about if the cancer came back? (This is particularly relevant for those who want to stop partway through treatment) | 1. Do they have an understanding that if the cancer comes back it invariably puts them in a worse situation than they are currently?<br><br>2. Do they understand the actual risk of it returning? For instance, if they are in their final treatment for low risk disease, this may look very different to if they have had one cycle of treatment for advanced disease.<br><br>3. Can they anticipate the anxiety that is inherent in the uncertainty about the likelihood of their cancer coming back? |

For those who have had multiple relapses or extended periods of time on treatment that may not have worked, many health professionals agree with the young person that it may not feel helpful to continue on a path that is not feeling productive, while also preventing them from spending 'quality' time doing things that they would want to do. For young people in this situation, the decision to stop treatment may be easier for the young person's family and all those around them, when compared to young people who are refusing treatment in the first instance. Young people may readily identify the sense of futility that they feel around perusing further active treatment, but may also speak about the sense of being compelled to continue by their parents, partners or health professional's expectations. Young people in this situation may need considerable support to help them identify what it would look like for them to be off treatment (as they may have been on treatment for years and have an unrealistic picture of what stopping would look like) as well as working with them to help communicate their decisions with not only their family, but also the treating teams.

> *Tyler is a 25-year-old who has been living with severe GVHD of the skin, digestive system and bladder for the year following his transplant for multiply relapsed leukaemia. She has been living with cancer for almost all her adult life and, due to complications, has been hospitalised for most of the last 18 months. She has very limited chance of recovering from her GVHD and has nearly died several times from infections and other complications, which have caused significant impairment to several of her major organs. Tyler decides that she wants to withdraw all treatment and die as she feels that she has suffered enough and is unlikely to either get better, or if she did, her quality of life would be much less than she would want.*

Although on a rational and practical level, the medical situations of young people such as Tyler provide straightforward answers in terms of the likelihood of her recovery. However, the decision to stop active management can be a very confronting issue for staff caring for the young person and their families. For someone like Tyler who has been on the ward for the last 18 months, the relationships built between the staff and the patient are often intense and highly intimate due to the level of personal care and time spent together. Staff can be very confronted by watching a relatively well young person come into the ward, who then gradually becomes more and more fragile and ultimately dies. This is particularly evident on wards where young patients have prolonged stays, but also in those wards where there are younger staff (those closer in age to the patient) as well as those who are the age of the parents of the young person. It is important that staff can identify appropriate supports and that support systems are facilitated with the guidance of the therapist, either via group or individual sessions, to help process the enormity of grief surrounding the loss of a young person, as well as the existential challenges for the staff.

At times, the decisions that young people may make for stopping treatment may seem unreasonable; however, underneath the surface there will generally be a further layer to what is happening. For instance, a young person with metastatic disease who makes the decision to stop chemotherapy as it is causing him neuropathy, but this is seen to be having some potential impact on his disease. On the surface his reasoning seems irrational, however, when he further explains that his neuropathy means he is unable to play his favourite video game anymore, and that is the only pleasure and connection he has left, that decision seems a little more reasonable. Some young people will make the decision to have quality over time, which many would argue is a very appropriate position.

# Chapter 15

# Competency

Competency is commonly talked about within psychology and psychiatry, however, it is often a misunderstood concept, particularly for those who are under the age of 18. In a general sense, competency is about establishing that a person can make a decision about their care based on processing and understanding the ramifications of this decision. For instance, establishing that a young person is able to make a decision about stopping treatment, and fully understand what it will mean to do so. For a person to be competent, they need to show that they are not experiencing any conditions or situations that are potentially impairing their decision-making, including medical conditions, influence of alcohol and other drugs, as well as significant mood or other psychiatric disorders. While there are similarities between the legal and commonly understood definitions there can also be significant differences.

To this end, this chapter is divided into two sections, content pertinent for those who are under 18, and those who are over 18. As it is not uncommon for patients under the age of 18 to be treated in adult hospitals, it may be helpful for those clinicians working in an adult setting to be familiar with the processes around competency for young people under 18, as when situations arise for these young people there may be few people in an organisation who are well versed in what to do to manage them.

## Under 18s

*Jenna is a 16-year-old with newly diagnosed acute
lymphoblastic leukaemia (ALL). She and her parents
have indicated that they do not want to have
chemotherapy as they believe that it will 'poison' her,
and instead, want to manage her ALL with a raw vegan
diet and solar therapy. Jenna is currently quite unwell,
as she had presented with quite advanced disease, and
is likely to die very quickly without some intervention.
Her parents have allowed her to have fluids, and Jenna
is refusing blood products, any chemotherapy and any
colony-stimulating medications. Her treating doctors
approach the medico-legal team at the hospital who
advise that they need to apply to the court to have her
treated for her disease, as it is in her best interests. The
court rules that she needs to have treatment, and is
ordered by the court to do so under duress.*

Although young people can consent to medical treatment at
the age of 16 in most states of Australia, the age of legal consent
is 18. Therefore, any decisions about ceasing treatment, or
establishing competence have specific rules applied to anyone
under the age of 18, regardless of their ability to consent for
medical treatment. The specific legal issues involved in establishing competence within a legal setting are extensive and
complex, and are not going to be described here. There have
been several well-documented cases of young people or their
families declining treatment, which when presented in a legal
context it was determined that it was in the young person's
best interests to have treatment, ultimately against their own
or their family's wishes. A situation such as this, of course, is
highly distressing for the young people themselves and also
for the treating teams, and the process can be highly divisive
across staff members.

Within children's hospitals, there will be clear protocols around the medico-legal requirements for managing a young person who declines treatment, particularly in the first instance. These processes will not be as clear within adult hospital and thus anyone who is managing a case such as this would be well advised to contact the medico-legal department of both the adult hospital, but also a paediatric-specific centre, which is more likely to have encountered these cases in the past. Furthermore, very detailed documentation needs to be completed, both to confirm a young person's ability to make decisions, but also if notes are subpoenaed and clinicians asked to present opinions about whether they believe the young person is competent. Ultimately, the court will decide about what the best course of action for a young person, based on the evidence presented by both the young person and their treating teams.

Regardless of the legal outcome or decision-making process, this time will be highly stressful for the young person, their family and all those involved in their care. The role of the therapist at this time is not just about assessing, and providing opinions about the young person and their understanding, but also to support everyone involved in the management of the situation, and the family through whatever the outcome of the situation may be. For those who are ultimately 'forced' into having treatment, young people and their families are likely to be quite distressed and angry, and find it very hard to manage. This will be particularly so if their reasons for not wanting treatment are culture- or religion-based, where there may also be significant ostracism from the community and support for having had this decision made legally. For those who are deemed able to make the decision about not having treatment, the implications and ramifications for this will also be significant, including on ward staff who may need to provide care for someone who may die from a potentially curable disease. Young people and their families are then likely to experience significant periods of grief and distress about the likely death. This will be especially pronounced when the parents of the young person had been advocating for treatment to be given, and this action not being taken. As mentioned in the previous chapter, the decision to cease treatment when a young person has already had significant interventions and been shown to have treatment-resistant disease will be much more straightforward, both legally and emotionally, compared to when a young person declines treatment for a potentially curable disease.

### Over 18

> *Pat, who is 20, presents to the emergency department with worsening headaches and lethargy and is found to have leukaemia. He has not practiced his religion for some years, but believes that it is a sin to have blood products, and he will be shunned by his community if he does so. When finding out that he will be unable to have treatment for his leukaemia without having blood product support, he makes the decision to not have treatment. He is assessed by both the psychologist and the psychiatrist who agree that he is fully understanding of the impact of his decision, and is not impacted cognitively. He has supportive care, including input from the palliative care team, and dies in hospital 4 weeks after his diagnosis.*

For those aged over 18, the process is much more straightforward and in some ways much easier to manage. Ultimately, once a young person turns 18, they can make decisions about their treatment, whether they have any treatment at all, and can decide to withdraw from treatment. That said, if there is any doubt about a young person's ability to make these decisions due to any factors related to mood, anxiety, treatment effects, neurocognitive concerns (including as a result of disease or treatment) or any other substance use, it is best to err on the side of caution to ensure that a thorough assessment of the young person is completed by a person external to the team. For those patients who have been well known to a therapist, although knowing them well and being able to engage around these issues, if there is concern about competency, a second opinion of someone who is neutral to the patient helps ensure that there is transparency in the process. This is particularly important if it is likely to require legal intervention. Legal intervention occurs considerably less frequently with young people who decide against treatment because most adults can make appropriate decisions when provided with information on which to base them.

For many young people who decide to stop treatment, these decisions will be based on a strong medical understanding of their situation and balanced by wanting to engage in activities that treatment may be preventing them from doing. Similarly, they may decide that the treatment is not working, or they may feel that they are ready to die. In these situations, there is very rarely a need for a formal competency assessment as these decisions are generally made in a rational way, and in consultation with their medical teams. This is less clear when the patients have not had treatment, or are refusing treatment for a potentially curable disease. In this instance, it is of paramount importance that clinicians and therapists are satisfied that the young person has an appropriate understanding of the ramifications of their actions.

Like those patients under 18, however, regardless of whether the young person decides to have treatment or not, they will require support in not only managing their own reactions to this, but also their support people's reactions.

Families will often struggle with the idea of a young person ceasing treatment, and will often be in a very different headspace around what ending treatment will mean, to that of the young person. Young people may need support in communicating their decisions about treatment to their peers, families and sometimes the teams caring for them.

## Chapter 16

# Anxiety in the Context of Cancer

---

'I had chemo six months ago, and I still can't think about drinking red PowerAde.'
— 19-year-old male

---

It stands to reason that young people having treatment for cancer are likely to become anxious. Most people have a sense of certainty around the ways in which the world works, however, the cancer process strips a sense of control, as well as providing ongoing anxiety-provoking situations. Treatment provides significant anxiety and inherent uncertainty as well as considerable discomfort.

Young people may not readily identify anxiety in the cancer setting, particularly if they have not previously experienced it. At times, it will be the people around them who will identify that the anxiety is a concern, rather than the young person themselves. This is particularly the case for young people who are in hospital for a long time and who may develop specific behaviours or difficulties coping with procedures or situations that arise. Nurses working with the young person may identify that a young person is having difficulty sleeping, or becoming fixated on particular aspects of their treatment that they have not been concerned about previously.

This chapter explores the commonly occurring anxiety symptoms that young people may experience in the context of their treatment. Although the focus is mainly on those anxieties that may become obvious during treatment, it is worth noting that anxiety is a common feature for many young people throughout their cancer experience, including around survivorship or recurrence (see chapters 18 and 20).

## Generalised Anxiety

As expected, for young people who have been diagnosed with cancer, there is an expectation that they will experience some anxiety about what is happening to them, regardless of whether this is around treatment, scans, uncertainty or a sense of the future. This expected anxiety around the above can sometimes become more generalised and start to impact on other aspects of the young person's world.

> 'Well, I got good scan results, but now I am worrying constantly about my relationship. Why can't my brain just stop worrying about everything.'
> — 21-year-old female

Within the cancer setting, it can feel easy to manage a young person's anxiety related to scans and cancer-related issues, whereas when they present with generalised anxiety they often seem much more difficult to manage. Therapists often report feeling that working with young people with generalised anxiety feels hard and overwhelming, which can be a mirror of the young person's experience of living with it. It is uncommon for young people to have not experienced any anxiety prior to the diagnosis to develop this kind of generalised anxiety. Thus, early assessment of premorbid anxiety can help to ascertain what the risk factors are for a young person to develop this kind of anxiety. Paradoxically, young people who will identify themselves as 'worriers' may often report that since the diagnosis they have not been feeling worried or overwhelmed about the cancer in the same way that they had worried about other things before. This, however, does not prevent the background worries about other aspects of their lives, including a fear about the future. This fear can be particularly prevalent in those who have had to put things on hold while having treatment, including university or relationships.

'Before the cancer, I was thinking all the time. I was worried about what my co-workers thought of me, and how I looked. Now I am bald and skinny, and I care about it, but not in the same way.'
— 23-year-old male

It is often helpful for young people to have these worries and generalised anxiety conceptualised in a couple of ways. Firstly, by identifying that they have always been a 'worrier' and that in the past this would have been helpful for them. It is unlikely that in the context of a stressor such as cancer that this is going to change right now (although they may be able to change it in the future), and for the moment this is about managing the worries, rather than trying to get rid of them. Secondly, by providing reassurance that although they may not be worried about the cancer, the cancer is making up a considerable part of their world and experience currently, which thus means that some of those worries and concerns exist within the parameters of their cancer experience. Finally, it is about allowing them to have a framework in which to conceptualise these worries and it is helpful to explain a therapeutic model in which they can use language and strategies to work with these worries.

Working within an ACT framework can be particularly helpful for managing the generalised anxiety that occurs around the cancer situation, as this can align nicely to the way that many of the other cancer issues are conceptualised. For instance, when working with thoughts and worries in the cancer context it is rarely helpful to engage in strict CBT strategies around thought-challenging, as these worries and thoughts are often based on a possible reality. However, young people work very well with the ideas of being able to notice thoughts, identifying them and making conscious efforts to not engage in them. If young people are also having difficulties with more generalised anxiety, they will be able to extend this framework into other thoughts and manage them in the same way (even if the content of the thoughts may be more abstract or unrealistic). It is important to note that those young people who have had long-term difficulties with generalised anxiety may have some crossover benefit from the interventions, specifically around managing cancer-related difficulties. This is particularly so if this includes interventions helpful in managing anxious thoughts, such as mindfulness skills and breathing training. While working with noncancer-specific thoughts, the therapist can use this framework to help bolster the ways in which young people work with any thoughts or worries, which will hopefully translate to improved anxiety management on completion of cancer-related therapy.

This generalised anxiety can become much more difficult to manage in the context of survivorship (see chapter 18 on survivorship) as there is much less certainty for the young person to work with as the routine of treatment is gone. There is also the sense that young people are 'cast out' into the world that can reactivate these worries and anxiety, not just about the survivorship-related thoughts, but thoughts about the rest of their lives. In some ways, this is a helpful time for this to happen as they are likely to still be well engaged with their therapist after completion of treatment (as opposed to many years post the completion of treatment) and will have increased capacity to put strategies into place that they may not have been able to manage while having treatment. For services with limits on the number of sessions that a young person can access after completion of treatment, it becomes important to transition that young person on to an appropriate therapist to manage the generalised anxiety if you do not have capacity to do so.

## Specific Phobias

Although not particularly common, from time to time young people may present with specific phobia which impacts on their ability to complete treatment. This can include aspects of medical care (such as needles or blood phobia) or can be related to the hospital itself (such as fear of nurses/germ phobias etc.). Although the recommended treatment in this instance would be to do standardised exposure therapy protocols, this can be problematic in this group for several reasons. Firstly, there is often not the time available to complete long exposure therapy treatment plans, with young people presenting unwell and needing to commence treatment quickly. Secondly, they are likely to be too overwhelmed at diagnosis to effectively engage in such protocols, with their focus on the processes around beginning treatment to effectively start psychological work and thirdly, with some medical phobias the young person may experience a significant vasovagal response (ie. Passing out) which may have already occurred multiple times prior to their referral to the therapy team, with the young people already having experienced difficult situations which results in an increase in anxiety. For managing these phobias, the process may be quite similar to those discussed in the chapter on anticipatory nausea and vomiting, including engaging sensory distraction, mindfulness strategies and at times the use of medications.

> *George is a 19 year old with Acute Leukaemia. He is*
> *required to have long hospital admissions as part of*
> *his treatment, however prior to his diagnosis he has*
> *experienced long standing germ phobias and anxiety*
> *which he has never sought treatment. At home he is able to*
> *manage these anxieties by controlling his environment and*
> *ensuring that he (and his family) wash their hands, clean*
> *multiple times per day as well as being able to keep his*
> *room very clean and ordered. However in his hospital room*
> *he has very little control over who comes in and out and*
> *what they touch, and has been told that he is at a very high*
> *risk of infection which has exacerbated his anxiety.*

Although this is an exceptional case, for someone like George treatment is even more difficult than for other young people. When a phobia or anxiety such as this is coupled with a difficult and unpredictable environment, as well as with medications such as steroids young people can become very overwhelmed very quickly. In someone like George it is unlikely to be helpful (or safe) to explore exposure work, instead the intervention is more likely to be around helping him manage the variables which are feeding his anxiety, and working with him to develop some tolerance strategies. Another key aspect of this management is around communication with the teams about George's situation and ways that they can support and manage his worries.

## Social Anxiety

For young people both in treatment and at the completion of treatment they may describe worries and anxieties around managing social engagements, even in those who appear to be socially confident and have broad social networks. For most young people this will manifest as worry about how they will communicate with their peers, and fear that they won't have anything of value to add to conversations or interactions due to their own focus on their illness. This can be particularly true of those who are spending most of their time in treatment or who have had significant changes to their body since they last spent time with their peers. Generally simple behavioural support strategies, and even role playing conversations with the young person will help manage this. Brainstorming with them around topics that they can talk about if they feel like they are running out of things to say, or conversation prompts are generally enough to help support them through this time. More often than not when the young person returns to their social group much of the anxiety will dissipate, if not, it would be appropriate to engage in a more formalised management program around social anxiety.

# Chapter 17

# Anticipatory Nausea and Vomiting

*Amber is an 18-year-old with leukaemia. She has completed all her intensive inpatient treatment and is now being managed as an outpatient. She has had her Hickman's line removed due to infection, and is having her treatment with cannulas currently. Over the last 3 treatments, the nurses in Day Therapy have noted that she has been increasingly nauseous and more difficult to cannulate. Her mum brings her to treatment and is concerned that she is becoming more withdrawn and nauseous in the days before treatment. On talking with Amber, she reports that she feels that she is managing well, but is 'sick of chemo' and is ready to go back to 'normal'.*

Amber's case is a very common situation for many young people undergoing chemotherapy. Anticipatory nausea and vomiting is well-documented within both paediatric and young adult populations with various schools of thought regarding the best treatment options. Within a clinical situation, it seems that those who have an access device (peripherally inserted central catheter [PICC], Hickman or Port-a-Cath) manage the impact of this considerably better, as patients report a reduced sense of anxiety around having to be cannulated. Placement of access devices are routine within paediatric hospitals, often used for patients who are having intensive chemotherapy regimes, however, for outpatients in the adult system they more commonly have treatment delivered via a cannula in a vein in their hand. These need to be inserted each treatment and can cause significant anxiety if a young person has difficulty with needles. Young people will often voice concerns regarding an access device, particularly those who may have a scar following the implantation. However, following implantation, their anxiety levels will often decrease significantly and they are able to better tolerate treatment. This is particularly important in young people who have a history of anxiety or needle phobias.

The symptoms experienced by young people associated with anticipatory nausea or vomiting can be hard to notice. For instance, they may start describing general feelings of nausea, or becoming more reluctant to come along to treatment. Generally, if you ask specific questions, young people will be able to identify at they are starting to feel nauseous on the day before, or morning of treatment. Young people may also talk about having difficulties being around objects or things that remind them of chemotherapy. For instance, young people who are given doxorubicin (a chemotherapy drug which is bright red) may become quite avoidant or feel nauseous when seeing something red that reminds them of the drug. Often young people will attribute all of the side effects of their chemotherapy to the 'red' drug simply due to its colour and the association for the young person. . Furthermore, if young people vomit on cannulation, this is significant sign that there is anticipatory anxiety. The young person might describe the anxiety building over the lead up to the time when they are going to be cannulated, but will report feeling better after vomiting.

Managing anticipatory anxiety and nausea in young p eople is often complex and multifactorial. Adding to the complication is the need for young people to have continuing exposure to the stressors of the treatment and for the triggers to be activated consistently. Below is a list of strategies that can be helpful in the management of the symptoms described above.

### 1. Identifying and naming the problem

Referring to the nausea or vomiting in the same terms as they would describe other aspects of being unwell makes the distinction and treatment of the symptoms harder to manage. However, if a young person can name and identify the symptoms accurately, they will be able to work with this in a more meaningful way. For instance, defining the nausea allows the young person to cognitively engage with the anxiety in a different way and, as such, can integrate existing CBT and ACT strategies. One of the easiest ways for young people to do this is to name the nausea something else, for instance simply calling it "hospital stomach" or "anticipation". By renaming it, both the therapist and the young person can work to identify the times when they are experiencing true nausea and when it is anxiety.

### 2. Working with the problem

Once the problem is identified — for instance, calling the nausea 'anticipation' the young person can work with it in a couple of ways. Often working within a problem-solving framework is effective as it allows the young person to feel some sense that the problem is manageable, unlike many of the other problems that exist during treatment.

In addition, there is evidence to suggest that the use of graded exposure is helpful for managing anticipatory nausea and vomiting. Clinical experience in this population has found, however, that this has proven quite troublesome primarily related to the time factor. Young people often have treatment frequently and are unwell between cycles (and even less keen than normal to attend the hospital). Setting up an environment where young people can have sustained graded exposure is very time-consuming and will often be sabotaged by unexpected admissions, reluctant participants, parents or other medical issues. However, aspects of graded exposure can be helpful, for instance, asking young people to engage in thoughts about treatment (outside of treatment) while engaging in relaxation/mindfulness strategies, or ensuring that they are not actively avoiding things that remind them of treatment.

### 3. Behavioural management

Ensuring some behavioural management strategies are in place helps the young person feel more able to control reactions, but are also useful in developing strategies for managing the periods of nausea, or anticipation both before and during treatment. Young people often naturally gravitate towards some of these strategies, such as those based around blocking out their environment and distracting themselves. It is important to help young people ensure that they do not create situations that will then have reminders of treatment onto other pleasurable aspects of their world, as the anticipatory cues are often highly transmissible to other situations. For instance, if they only listen to a particular music album while in chemotherapy/hospital, the association will become significant, and the music itself will evoke anticipatory anxiety. Some of the strategies which young people can use are those which disconnect them from the triggers in the environment such as spraying a strong perfume on their sleeve that they can smell to override the 'hospital smell', listening to music via headphones to block out the noises of the unit or wearing sunglasses/sitting with eyes closed.

### 4. Medications

For young people who are unable to engage in the above strategies for any reason, including medical issues, medications may often be the only option for managing the anticipatory nausea and vomiting, particularly if it is likely to prevent a young person from continuing treatment. Short-acting benzodiazepines are often used in a chemotherapy setting for the management of nausea, and work particularly well in managing anticipatory nausea. Often the reaction will be triggered as early as getting in the car to come to the hospital, or as soon as the young person starts packing their 'hospital bag' so it is often ineffective to wait to use the medication until they are just about to start treatment. Instead, advising the young person to take a dose in the morning before they leave for the hospital, or on the way in, will help them be more relaxed on arrival and hopefully break some of the immediate association on attending the hospital. Of course, there can be significant long term implications of long term benzodiazepine use and so it would be appropriate to have a plan to manage this, preferably in consultation with the psychiatry team, however in my experience with young people this has rarely been an issue.

Chapter 18

# Survivorship

'It's actually harder for me now that I am better than it was during treatment.'
— 19-year-old woman

Within the oncology population broadly, the emotional and psychological challenges of completing treatment, and transitioning back to 'normal life' have been well established. This also holds true for young people who will often report significant challenges in regaining a sense of normality and reintegrating into their 'old' lives.

> Jane is a 22-year-old woman who had treatment for Ewing's sarcoma, including chemotherapy and surgery that has resulted in changes in her mobility and function of her left knee. Prior to her diagnosis, she had been working as a retail assistant while attending university to become a nurse. She has been unable to return to work due to being unable to stand for long periods, and is now having to evaluate whether it is reasonable for her to continue her nursing studies. She has missed a year of university due to treatment and all her peer group has now graduated.

Jane's situation is a particularly common one, with young people often being 'left behind' by their peers and the people around them, which often becomes more evident when having to reintegrate into their pre-cancer lives than it had been when they had been in treatment. Furthermore, young people will often report feeling unprepared for what it will be like to finish treatment and the anxiety and worry which can accompany this.

For many people, the completion of treatment and beginning to restart activities signals that the cancer is over, with the assumption that the young person is no longer impacted by the significance of what has happened. This is reinforced by the young person starting to look like their 'old selves' again, including regaining hair, gaining or losing weight, and improving mobility (among those who have had treatment that has impacted function). From the outside looking in, the logical conclusion for most people surrounding the young person that they are 'normal' again, and all the concessions they had been afforded while unwell disappear, and expectations about their ability to complete roles and tasks reappear. However, for the young person themselves, this can be a tumultuous time filled with fear, anxiety, uncertainty and difficulties in managing their mood.

### Making sense of what just happened

'It's like I was dreaming all the way through chemo, and then just like that, I have woken up. But life now feels very scary'.
— 19-year-old male

During treatment, young people often feel like they are trapped between cycles, simply living from one chemotherapy treatment or procedure to the next. Young people will often speak about 'writing off' periods of time following each treatment, and can accurately predict when they will have energy or motivation to manage engagement with their peers, or to attend work or school. These cycles, albeit unpleasant, become the foundations for making sense of what is happening, and predictive in their lives while they are on treatment. Being on treatment also provides considerable comfort and reinforcement by having contact with health professionals and regular check-ins to see how they are going both medically and psychologically. During treatment, young people will report a sense of urgency to have treatment completed, while at the same time feeling quite settled in the process. Psychologically, it is generally not helpful for people to try and focus too much on the enormity of what is happening while they are in treatment, and particularly in pondering the existential implications of such.

> 'I knew treatment was bad, but after treatment is much worse'.
> — 16-year-old female

On completion of treatment, however, young people are often faced with the colossal psychological task of making sense of all of things that have happened to them over the preceding weeks/months. It is at this time that young people have space to engage in thoughts about the bigger picture implications of their cancer and the treatment, including issues around fertility preservation, late effects, chemotherapy, surgical implications, and general fears/concerns about their cancer returning. This is when young people are at risk of developing anxiety and low mood in the context of uncertainty and being consciously aware (often for the first time in their lives) that they do not know what the future may hold.

> 'I could have died, I knew it at the time, but when I think about it now .... I could not be here'.
> — 25-year-old male

One of the biggest challenges inherent within the cancer process for most patients, and those around them, is the sense of mortality and the risk that the cancer poses. Unconsciously, as human beings we will have connections between cancer and death, whether they be from examples in our lives, or from references within popular culture and media. We know that when a patient is given the diagnosis of cancer they often fail to hear or process any further information provided to them in a consultation, as they and their brains try to make sense of the implications and potential impact of the diagnosis. Young patients are not exempt from this and, on completion of treatment, the reality of the potential outcomes of the disease are realised and can result in a stocktake of their lives and the meaning of what is within them.

Developmentally, within adolescence and young adulthood young people are at a time in their lives when they feel invincible and infallible. Cancer provides a stark contrast to this perception and profoundly challenges the young person's sense of identity and meaning. When this is paired with the natural curiosity about death and mortality that occurs for young people in their late adolescence, young people are often well-equipped and willing to explore these concepts in ways that adults often are unable to process.

Working with young people who are engaging in thought and wonder about their sense of mortality and existential meaning can be challenging but rewarding work to engage in. One of the challenges for young people at the end of treatment is that they are often given signals that it is not okay to talk about the cancer anymore, and that any talk of the cancer is almost inviting the cancer back. Generally, young people will relish the opportunity to speak openly about their own mortality and the fears and worries that they have about the future. This includes discussion about making meaning in the future, and how they might feel different to how they had been before the cancer.

> 'I used to be an asshole. I would go out, get smashed and pick fights with anyone. I know now that I was just scared of what

people thought, and actually I don't need to be like that'.
— 18-year-old.

Often, as the young person gets further from their treatment, they are less likely to focus on the minutiae of the treatment itself, but instead focus on the 'bigger picture' meaning of what the cancer has meant for them. Whereas immediately following treatment the discussions around the cancer are likely to be more focused on the specifics and effects (generally the negative ones) about how they can ever be as they were after having these things happen to them. Initially, young people may be quite closed to discussions about the future and how they can make sense of it, but this may change as they become physically better and can see that changes can happen for them, even though they may feel frustratingly slow!

Sometimes young people respond well to gentle prompting around exploring the ways that the cancer has changed them, for instance, 'how do you think you would have thought about that before the cancer?' or 'It sounds like you think about _____ differently now'. Additionally, young people will often require significant reassurance and validation that it is okay for them to be finding the adjustment back to 'normal' hard. It can be helpful to work with them around what they would like their 'normal' to be now, while also recognising that they can and may need to be different.

It can be around some of these difficulties that ACT-based strategies, particularly related to stopping the struggle, can be helpful. For instance, in Jane's case it can be helpful for her to examine the grief and difficulties that she has around the loss of her function, career, as well as her imagined future. In conjunction with the grief, it would be helpful for her to work with the concept of accepting the change in her function, and working with her to help overcome the cognitions and thoughts causing her distress around the grief itself.

## What it means to live with uncertainty

One of the most difficult aspects of finishing treatment and moving into the 'survivorship' phase is learning how to make sense of having to live with uncertainty. Prior to a diagnosis, uncertainty is a not something that most people, especially young people, have considered even though it is a consistent feature of life. Once the cancer has become part of a person's life, they become acutely aware of the impact of the uncertainty, often questioning the sense of 'normal' and making sense of meaning for the future.

> *Michael, is a 26-year-old who has recently finished treatment for* non-Hodgkin lymphoma *(NHL). He has been told that he has the 'all clear' for now, but is aware that his cancer will more than likely return. He wants to go and travel and feels that he needs to 'reclaim' the time he lost during treatment, but at the same time is paralysed with fear that the cancer will come back. He reports that he is so anxious about what will happen if the cancer comes back, that he has been reading everything that he can find about the type of lymphoma he has, and has been unable to think about anything else. His sleep has been disrupted because of this, and he can't spend time with his friends as he feels like they don't understand.*

For many patients, this sense of uncertainty about the future can result in a generalised anxiety about making decisions and engaging in activities (such as booking holidays, committing to jobs or relationships). Much of the uncertainty that young people face in the context of their cancer is related to whether the cancer will return. Post-diagnosis, young people will often speak about the sense that they cannot trust their bodies, nor trust the sense of future. Any decision can take on a new meaning in the context of not knowing whether the cancer may or may not returning, and not knowing whether things that had been reliable predictors in the past can be used in the future.

It is almost impossible for young people to find people around them who have a good understanding of what living with this uncertainty is like, unless they meet another young person who has already been through a similar experience. There is often significant stigma and reluctance to engage in discussions about relapse with people around them, often leaving young people feeling isolated in their sense of uncertainty and concern about the future. Often one of the most helpful things that can be done when working with a young person who is finding the uncertainty difficult to manage is to allow them to give space to the feelings and emotions that come with it. Often, by talking about it and normalising the experience, young people can make sense of their emotions and can acknowledge that the 'foreignness' of this experience is okay and in time it will be manageable. Generally, the further that the young person gets away from treatment, and the more good results they have, the more the uncertainty fades, although it is unlikely that it will ever resolve completely.

One of the most helpful strategies for managing the sense of uncertainty is trying to put some parameters around it. Although this seems like a ridiculous premise given the inability to define or reduce the uncertainty by its very nature, there is often a benefit in exploring how one might reduce the sense of uncertainty.

### Steps in managing the uncertainty
### 1. What is the young person fearful of?
For most young people, this will generally be around relapse, a sense of worry about the future and how they will function,

decisions about relationships and fertility, and their sense of mortality.

### 2. Are there things that would allay their fears or concerns?

For some of the concerns described above it will be very difficult to allay uncertainty and fear completely, particularly in the context of fear of death or seemingly unfixable situations. For many young people, actually naming the fear allows them to begin to change their relationship to it and build strategies that would make the fear feel more manageable. For instance, often people will talk about feeling better if they know there is a plan if the cancer were to return, or that there are strategies that can be used so they are not in pain. Even talking about these things in an abstract sense can help manage the underlying fear.

### 3. Writing a fear plan

Ask the young person to write down examples or strategies that they can use to allay their fears and uncertainty. Explain to them that they can use this as a reference point for when the thoughts may come into their mind, or if they are finding it hard to manage a particular worry.

Below is an example of a fear plan for Michael. It is noted that the reassuring thoughts are generic, but the goal is for the young person to be able to connect with these thoughts when the worries about the future appear. The young person can aim to identify more specific thoughts to manage this than they are currently able to, however, for most, a general sense of knowing that there is a plan for how to manage their worries then it will almost immediately feel more manageable.

## Table 18.1

| Fear | Thoughts around Fear | Emotions | Reassuring Thoughts |
|------|---------------------|----------|---------------------|
| Recurrence | 1. If my cancer comes back, it is going to be much worse, and I think I will die. 2. I will die in horrible pain | 1. Fear 2. Distress 3. Anxiety 4. Low Mood | 1. I am not sure what the treatment will be, but I know that there is another treatment available. 2. I trust my doctor, and I know that she will tell me if I need to worry 3. There are multiple pain management strategies that I can use if I need them. |

### 4. Normalise the recurrence of these thoughts

Even with a documented sense of plan, it is unlikely that these thoughts will disappear forever. Spend time talking with the young person about how to anticipate when these worries and thoughts may emerge, but also about how to tap into the strategies that they have used in the past to manage the thoughts. This includes helping them to identify times that are most likely to cause recurrence of thoughts, such as around scan times or coinciding with big life events for themselves or other people.

It's important that the young person has a sense of control over the relationship with uncertainty, including that the goal of working with the thoughts is not about removing the uncertainty, as this is impossible in the context of the cancer. Generally, once young people can work with this concept, they are better equipped to sit with the uncertainty and engage in strategies to help manage it.

Chapter 19

# Scan Anxiety

Scans and check-ups can become a double-edged sword for many young people. They provide reassurance and reconnection with the hospital, of course, but can be a source of significant anxiety. They can also be a reminder that they have been unwell in the past and there is a chance that they may become unwell again in the future. It is not uncommon in the lead-up to the period of scanning that young people will become acutely anxious, have ruminations about relapse and find it almost impossible to think about anything else. The time frames for this to occur may not be predictable, and may not happen in the first or second periods following the completion of treatment. Of course, those young people who have had significant other stressors in their lives will be more prone to anxiety around scans and results than their counterparts who are less under pressure.

For some, the anxiety is not limited to the period leading up to scans, and they may find themselves preoccupied with any sensation in their body as being a sign of relapse. This can, of course, be a self-perpetuating cycle with increasing anxiety becoming evident in physiological manifestations, which in turn increase the young person's anxiety about what is happening to them and becoming more and more convinced of their relapse. This anxiety can also manifest in persistent thought and worry about the cancer, and fixation on their cancer journey. Patients experiencing this difficulty are also less likely to re-engage in their normal activities, or find themselves unable to engage and be present in activities due to the thoughts about the relapse.

> 'All I can think about is the cancer coming back, maybe if I think about it enough, I will be prepared properly this time when it happens'.
> — 19-year-old woman

In some ways, there is utility in this way of thinking. For most young patients, their diagnosis had come without warning, and generally attracted considerable feedback about the unlikely nature of their diagnosis. For instance, the well-intentioned comments of 'But, you are so young!' which will often accompany news of diagnosis and treatment. Many young people speak openly about having a sense that they need to be prepared for when the cancer comes back, and go into appointments with the expectation that the results will be bad. This can be a helpful strategy to the extent that the young person feels prepared, and often they will likely get good results and have their method of coping reinforced. In addition, there can be a sense of security in feeling that by anticipating potential relapse, the reality of managing it will also feel okay, which of course is not as straightforward psychologically as it first appears (see chapter 20 on recurrence). Some choose to engage in the opposite method, by assuming that everything will be fine, which is also generally reinforced. There are, of course, situations where this is not the case and this can lead to significant psychological distress and panic if the patient was fully committed to the idea that they would get good results. Ideally there is the middle ground, where young people have conceptualised (as much as possible) both potential outcomes and have emotional strategies prepared for both scenarios. The ongoing scans and reviews will happen for at least five years for most patients, and so developing good strategies to manage these early on can lead to a noticeable reduction in anxiety and distress for these young people.

Over time, as expected, the intensity of the reactions to knowing that scans or reviews are coming up tend to reduce somewhat, but it is unlikely that these sensations will ever disappear completely. It is important to prepare the young person for this and preliminary discussions about what to expect from entering the surveillance period can start before treatment has been completed. This allows the young person to start thinking about what it will be like to stop treatment, and reduce contact, but also normalise the experience of anxiety and apprehension around scans, and the implications of this on their function. Some of the most helpful strategies that can be employed at this time allow young people to prepare and be aware of what the survivorship period will look like, which ultimately provides a reference point for them around how to anticipate their anxiety and uncertainty.

> *Thomas is a 19-year-old who had recently completed treatment for testicular cancer. He managed very well during treatment and did not have any anxiety. However, since completing treatment, he reports that he has become 'obsessed' with his cancer coming back, and has had several presentations to the clinic with body pain and generalised symptoms such as fatigue and low appetite. He reports that he knows that even if his cancer came back his overall prognosis would be quite good, but he worries that he might not be able to tolerate having more chemotherapy. He reports that he knows that he probably hasn't relapsed, but worries about everything that happens in his body.*

For those who experience significant body-focused and gener-alised anxiety in the lead-up to scans it can be helpful to help put parameters around the symptoms. For instance, providing psycho-education about how to manage thoughts around body experiences. In the case of Thomas, it would be useful to help him put some limitations around engagement with these sensations, including setting rules about when he can seek out medical attention, for example, 'if the pain is still there in 3 days I will go to the doctor'. If the young person can be distracted from their pain, or it becomes particularly evident when they are more anxious, there may be a significant component of anxiety involved. However, young people do relapse and so it is important to encourage them to be reviewed if there are concerns for them medically, or if they have persistent symptoms. By providing young people with a psycho-education framework about why they are reacting in the way that they are, it allows them to work with the sensations as well as in the way that they manage their thoughts around the relapse itself.

> 'I just can't trust my body anymore, and I know if it comes back, I am f*&ked'.
> — 23-year-old male

Of course, the anxiety around scans is very reasonable as these young people will have had a bad scan or results in the past. Potentially, the last scan they had was the one that heralded the cancer into their world. Most people are very aware that if they are to relapse, the cancer is much more difficult to manage medically, and could mean that their prognosis is much poorer than it was initially (see chapter 20 on recurrence). The stakes are high around why they are anxious, and thus challenging these worries is generally quite ineffective. Instead, young people will generally find it more helpful to work with these thoughts towards managing them, rather than trying to get rid of them, or provide opposition to such. It can be helpful to work with a problem-solving model so that there is a sense of control over the situation that allows a sense of a plan to be completed. This remains effective even if the plan itself changes. Similar to the plans discussed regarding fear of relapse, strategies can be used as reinforcements to help the young person manage their fear while also providing a framework around discussing their worries and fears about the future.

Although it seems improbable, some young people have the sense that they are not only going to relapse, but also will speak about knowing that they were always going to get cancer, and having a sense that they will not live very long. Expectantly, for those who have accurately predicted their cancer, they can become quite worried and anxious if they start to feel they are going to relapse. Unfortunately, for many of the young people who feel this way, the cancer does return and this can be difficult for them to manage. There is no explanation as to why this occurs, and why they have this awareness, however, it is very important to support them within these fears rather than disregard them. Often clinicians, when lacking evidence for particular things, can be suspicious of their validity, and if young people are treated in this way they can disengage from the clinician easily, as often the rest of their network will also be disregarding their concerns.

# Chapter 20

# Recurrence

Recurrence for any patient is devastating, even if it has been anticipated. Every young person who has been through the cancer process is acutely aware that there is always a risk that it can come back. Some are also aware that if it comes back the condition is much more difficult to manage, and many will perceive recurrence as the beginning of the end. For others, they may be blissfully unaware of the physiological and psychological impacts of the recurrence, and the impact of re-embarking on treatment.

For some, the recurrence will be completely unexpected, such as those who have recurrence found during routine scans or 3-monthly check-ups. Others will report a sense of knowing that there were going to recurrence and of awaiting the time when that would occur. Even in the context of this 'knowing' the reality of what this looks like can be shocking and young people will indicate that even though they knew it was going to happen, they had been secretly hoping that it wouldn't be the case. The other group of young people are those who are told from the beginning that their disease is likely to return. These patients are sometimes able to rationalise that reality and prepare themselves at every scan that this may occur. Just as often, however, young people will have told themselves that it wouldn't happen to them, and are genuinely shocked when it occurs. Young people are never going to respond to recurrence in a consistent or predictable way, and most of the work done with young people around this time is based on the existing therapeutic relationship and connecting with the skills and tools that they have been able to use in the past. For those therapists who are meeting a young person for the first time following recurrence, it presents a difficult therapeutic space to occupy, with the chance of limited engagement by the young person themselves, reduced capacity to do anything that is likely to have improvement in a short period of time, and difficulties in engaging young people in conversations around existential matters when they are not comfortable or trusting in the relationship.

As mentioned in previous chapters, the therapeutic space is often where young people feel free and supported to be able to discuss the uncertainty about their future and worries about what would happen should their disease return. The period of recurrence often exacerbates this further, as expected, and can lead to young people pursuing conversations around the potential ending of their lives, and worries about if they were to deteriorate and die. This is normal in the context of these events; however, these conversations can be quite distressing for clinicians. The recurrence can prompt a further evaluation of the young person's life, including whether they wish to have further treatment, of what would they would like the remaining time left to look like if they were to die. For some young people with recurrenced disease, their prognosis remains very good and very likely to be cured, whereas for others a recurrence can move their disease from the 'curable' category to the 'terminal' category, although it is important to note it is rarely spoken about in these terms with young people.

In those who continue to have a good prognosis even in the context of recurrence, for them the adjustment to recurrence might look quite different, and may mirror the frustrations common in the context of treatment. This is particularly true in those who have not had much time between completion of treatment and recurrence, as the memories of what it was like to be on treatment remain very salient. For these patients, the focus of psychological treatment is more about engaging them in how they are going to manage treatment again, and the frustrations of life 'getting back to normal' only to have it put on hold again for further intervention. Although this will affect both groups of patients, those who are more significantly unwell may focus on this differently. Patients with recurrence that remains curable may have what they will perceive as mixed messages from the people around them, including their team. They may be having communication about recurrence (which for most patients is what they are ultimately fearing) in a way that suggests that it is very manageable and fixable, to the point where it might feel like an extension of what has already occurred. The young person may feel very different about this and may report a sense that their fears and worries are being minimised by the team and their family. Often the therapeutic space will remain where they are able to articulate this fear, and work through the challenge of managing the very real threat to their mortality.

The patients who have a dire disease course following recurrence are also likely to identify the above as challenges, particularly in relation to how they perceive the people around them making sense of their recurrence, and the language around it used by their treating team. They are generally terrified about what the outlook may be for them and become frustrated by the ongoing sense of uncertainty around their disease and its process. Furthermore, being able to make decisions about what needs to happen for them can feel quite overwhelming, particularly for those patients who have options with uncertain outcomes. For instance, the patient offered a trial drug or a treatment protocol by a clinician as an option, but being unable to give specific answers around what the likely success or failure rates of the treatment may be. This scenario is more likely to occur for those young people who have recurred on several occasions, and they may have different ways of coping with this information to those who are recently recurred, but will still reliably find the uncertainty difficult to manage.

> 'I guess I will just live with this s*&t forever'.
> — 21-year-old man with metastatic sarcoma

The patients who are attending sessions following recurrence may be quite keen to speak about its impact, but as in the case of new diagnosis, it is not helpful to review someone until several days following the news, to allow them space to process this information for themselves. It is important for young people to have this time, and around the time of recurrence, repeated requests may come for the young person to be reviewed. These requests for review are much more likely to be about the team and family's anxiety, rather than the young person themselves. At this time, young people are expected to be anxious, angry, frustrated, distressed, depressed, teary, withdrawn and speaking morbidly about their future. These emotions, although normal can be quite concerning for the team caring for the young person, but it is important that clinicians have strategies to manage their own distress in relation to these issues, and to allow the young person to grieve their potential loss of future (both short- and long-term). These acute mood changes are generally short-lived, and can be reduced by the young person having a clear plan of what is going to happen next. Even if the situation presented is quite dire, they will have a better ability to manage the certainty inherently involved in such, rather than having to sit with the uncertainty of knowing that the disease has returned, but not knowing what it means for them. Changes in mood will also be sustained and perpetuated by physical discomfort, pain, difficulties sleeping (usually in a ward environment) or being unwell, so it is important that these things are also managed well prior to review, or if reviews occur during this time, these symptoms are addressed accordingly. It is crucial at this time that young people are the drivers in engagement with their therapist, choosing to have sessions or not may be one of the only things that they can have agency over in this time of uncertainty.

In the early stages of recurrence, young people may be reluctant to speak about the recurrence or its potential implications and may revisit the earlier discussions that feature ideas and thoughts around acceptance, for instance 'what can I do?' or 'I guess I will just have more chemo'. Even though the young person may appear to have disengaged from the relationship, it is more likely to do with processing the information, and they will reconnect as the reality of living with the recurrence becomes more easily accessible for them to talk about. During the initial stages, the strategies that tend to be helpful are those which tap into the difficulties they identify as problems in moving forward. These may include, for instance, managing being back in the inpatient setting, having to recommence treatment, taking more time out from university or talking with their friends about the recurrence. As the therapist who has been engaged with the young person for some time (although there may have been an absence since you last saw them) the young person should connect with you quite well around this as it is familiar territory, and the strategies are easy for them to implement. If this is not the case, and you are meeting them for the first time, then to build engagement and support with the young person the strategies likely to have the most immediate impact are the best place to start. For instance, those around managing anxiety in hospital, or how to talk with their friends. Young people who have had lots of exposure to the health setting will generally find that their tolerance to all things medical will have decreased significantly by the time that they are 'back' for further treatment, which may be reflected in how they engage with the staff around them, as well as treatment itself. Young people are more familiar with the medical setting itself, and the medications, so might be more likely to stipulate what drugs they are reluctant to have, ways that they want things administered, and raise concerns about what is happening more frequently than they would have initially. This can be particularly evident in patients who are more anxious, or have been away from the hospital for an extended period. For those who have had little time between completion of treatment and recurrence, they will undoubtedly be unhappy about having to restart treatment, but will adapt to treatment and the routine of such much faster than those who have been away for a longer period.

A slight aside, but it is important to note that those who have had treatment for a paediatric cancer in the children's hospital and then go on to have treatment in an adult setting will usually have quite complex adjustment issues to the new hospital, as well as having to manage the implications of either recurrence or a second cancer. The way that children make sense of their cancer experience is different to that of adults and young adults, for obvious developmental reasons, and may have trauma-related responses to their experience of treatment when they were younger. Although these issues are not going to be addressed here, it is important to be mindful of the potential 're-triggering' of trauma experiences that may occur as these young people enter treatment.

As young people move into the restarting of treatment and have some certainty of a plan around what is going to happen in this context, the issues around the 'bigger picture' and existential nature of having recurred may become more of a focus. Therapeutically, these patients tend to respond well to more existential-based discussions at this time and work around the management of their emotions and worries around their future. It can be helpful to work with young people around the notion of 'grief', and this can help them identify what the cancer has taken away, or what it might take away from them. Some young people will not require this level of prompting about his, and will feel very comfortable speaking about their worries about dying, and the challenges managing their fear of mortality. As mentioned previously, the ACT framework can be useful for these concerns, and gently suggesting ways in which the young person can manage any practical anxieties that they may have, for instance, needing to make wills, legacy making, making sense of what they might need to resolve should something happen to them. Incorporating some aspects of concrete action in which they can engage can alleviate the intensity of the existential uncertainty, although of course it will not remove it in any sense.

# Chapter 21

# Engagement of palliative care

For many health professionals, the mere mention of the word 'palliative care' signals imagery of a white flag being raised to the disease and certainty of death. Although the palliative care team is often used to manage end-of-life symptoms and complications, palliative care can also be engaged early in the treatment process to help young people manage the symptoms of tumours, side effects of chemotherapy and supportive care. Importantly, as with the relationship of a young person with the therapist, developing and fostering the relationship with the palliative care physician early on allows ongoing engagement and management. This is a stark contrast to waiting until the proverbial '11th hour' where the young person and their family are likely to have significant difficulties in engagement, which is very much about symptoms rather than holistic care.

> 'I really like working with Dr.... [Palliative Care], as long as I don't have to call her. Her admin person also answers the phone with "Hello, Palliative Care Department". I just have to pretend that my doctor is a special doctor in that team. She manages my pain, that's all.'
> — 18-year-old female

Within teams where the engagement of palliative care occurs for any young people who have presented with advanced disease, or significant symptom burden, the patients are generally accepting of the 'pain management doctors' without opposition. However, if the notion of the 'palliative care team' is not discussed until the young person has been given poor prognosis information then they are much more likely to be reluctant and hard to engage around these issues, even if symptom control occurs. Interestingly, although teams may identify reluctance around what being referred to palliative care will mean for patients and their families, if they are provided with an appropriate framework then young people can make sense of this and are open to the support provided. Using language perceived as less threatening, such as calling the team the 'symptom management team' or 'pain management team' can be helpful; although young people will often identify which team they are dealing with when they are contacting the offices for appointments and other administrative issues.

If there is a conscious transition from active to palliative care, the young person and their family will often note the change, even if this isn't announced in any formal way. For instance, they may note that the palliative care team are now making more decisions than previously, or their consultant oncologist may still come around, but much less frequently. This is often a time of grief for the patients and their families for several reasons. These changes signal a very real and tangible marker that things have changed and the young person is deteriorating. Furthermore, there can be grief about the transition itself and the loss of the relationship with the person who has provided their care since the beginning. Of course, ideally both teams would stay engaged with the patient to allow this sense of continuity of care, as well as to reduce the patient's perception of feeling abandoned. If this occurs it is of paramount importance to ensure that all channels of communication are clear to prevent any risk of mixed messages or conflicting information being given to the patient.

For those young people who have not had active engagement with palliative care from early on in their diagnosis, or for those who are meeting them while treatment is being withdrawn, or medical complications are occurring, the fear around an unfamiliar team is difficult to manage. This is, of course, amplified by the knowledge that the role of the palliative care team at this time is likely to be a consistent presence up to the young person's death. Therapists can be an integral part of this transition in several ways. Firstly, as the person well known to the family and young person there is an existing relationship that allows difficult conversations about the end of life nearing and the role of palliative care. These conversations can introduce concepts of symptom management, but also explore fears and worries about what the young person feels about dying, and what they want to happen at this time. Family members are also able to express fears and distress to someone who is familiar. Secondly, the therapist can provide a bridge between the oncology/ haematology team and the palliative care team, which can be particularly important if the treating team is going to change. This can be facilitated well in situations where the therapist is present in medical consults with the young person, and they can be the constant in these consults (where appropriate), but they can also support the young person in understanding information that they may be hearing for the first time.

If the facility and schedules allow, it can be a useful intervention for the therapist (or appropriate support person) to be present in the medical consults, if not consistently, on an occasional basis or if pivotal information is going to be provided. This is most important if the young person comes to appointments alone, and does not have a good support network. The therapist can be a 'translator' of information between the team and the young person, and provide a context for decisions made in particular ways. This also means that when a change in treatment, or deterioration occurs, it is easier for the therapist to be present in that space to support the young person and their family. Young people will often want to debrief following medical consults and find it helpful to have another person present who heard the same information as them. This information can also facilitate discussions if a young person has misunderstood information, which may be especially evident if there is a change in prognosis.

Chapter 22

# Building a Legacy

One of the things that young people will often speak about at the end of life is an incredible expectation on them to be able to leave a legacy and make their time important. Some of these expectations come from within and some externally, but regardless of their origin they can be paralysing for the young person facing their mortality, particularly when unwell. Culturally, there are multiple references around what 'dying young' is meant to mean and most refer to extraordinary and often unobtainable expectations. For instance, members of the '27 club' (celebrities who die on or before their 27th birthday), notable cancer figures the concepts around 'bucket lists' and works of fiction (for example, *The Fault in Our Stars*). Most young people, particularly those who are dying, do not have capacity or the options to engage in extraordinary feat, they can become overwhelmed and paralysed by what they are 'meant to be doing'.

> 'I think I have well and truly missed my opportunity for greatness, I now just want enough energy to spend time with my friends. Maybe even go to the pub.'
> — 18-year-old male

Furthermore, there are often expectations about what young people 'should' be able to do with the time that they have left. At times, these things can be relevant and helpful — for instance, a young person's friends buying them tickets to do something that they have always wanted to do, or help supporting a young person to do something that is meaningful for them. These things can be incredibly simple, yet incredibly significant. Young people often don't feel these extreme activities are helpful at this time, and they may not have the capacity to do these in the way that they would like. As such, the fantasy of what that might have looked and felt like, had they have been well, is a much more satisfying space for them to sit with. Similarly, relationships become much more meaningful, as do the simple things that are taken away through the treatment process, like being able to sit in the sun, or go to the pub with a friend.

> 'I had been playing online games with him for years, and I thought that I would never meet him now. He made it happen though.'
> —19-year-old male

Less-helpful suggestions are often those driven by other people. For instance, a 16-year-old who has been offered a 'Make A Wish' receiving suggestions that he should go on a family trip to Disneyland; or a 23-year-old woman who was encouraged to return to a third world country to be closer to her family, but who wanted to remain in Australia with her care team. Young patients can be bombarded with well-intentioned suggestions about what they 'need' to do, including making future legacy-based activities, such as leaving cards for each of their younger sibling's birthdays, video journals of their death, or chronicling how they feel about all the people in their world. Although, these are good ideas, they are emotionally and physically difficult to manage with limited resources. Patients need to be feeling very resilient and well before attempting any of these things with most being abandoned due to the confronting nature of conceptualising the world without them present in it. It is a difficult ask for anyone to be able to take the relatively abstract idea of the world continuing following your own death; this does not change for young people and, in some ways, it is even more challenging due to their pervasive sense of self, even in the face of very real threats to their mortality.

> 'I could clean out my room, and all of my stuff. But then I think, well I don't want to do it really, and it's not like it's going to be my problem.'
> — 23-year-old male

The way that young people respond to being presented with a very limited life expectancy can vary tremendously. Some may stick their head firmly in the sand and refuse to discuss or conceptualise anything about what may happen in the lead-up to their death, or following. Others will organise everything about the end of their lives, including where they want to die, how alert they want to be, as well as what will happen following their death — such as where their belongings go and how they want to be remembered. It is important to note that even if they have decided to not actively engage in discussions about this does not mean that they are in denial or not accepting their prognosis. Instead, it may be that they have done as much thinking and talking about it as they need to do; it is often these patients that have very well-considered plans about what they want to happen as they deteriorate and decisions must be made about their care.

As the therapist working with young people at this stage of their lives, the work that can be done is pivotal, but it often very confronting. Discussion of the practicalities of a young person's end of life and what they leave behind can provoke very strong emotions, not only for the patient but also for the therapist. Generally, these conversations will lead to reflection on the therapist's own beliefs about where they are in relation to the patient's wishes, which may elicit strong positive and negative emotions. There is often significant anxiety within teams and families for young people to have an acceptance of their death, which can lead to pressure on the therapist to make the young person talk and ultimately resolve any unresolved 'things' prior to their death. There will always be unresolved 'things', as that is the nature of human beings. Young people need to be the drivers of any discussions about time at their end of life and the meaning that they wish to make about it. Some will speak about this in every session for the time that they have left, whereas others will only ever speak about it once, and feel that they have said all that needs to be said. It is not the job of the therapist to 'uncover' something, sometimes things are just as they are and a young person will die without ever confronting or managing things that perhaps those around them think they should.

> 'I have the list of things that I need to give to people. I know exactly where everything is going. Except, whenever I try and give the stuff to them, and say goodbye, they tell me to stop it, and tell me that I need to think positive. Like somehow by communicating about me dying might make it actually happen.'
> — 22-year-old female

The inverse of those who believe that young people should spend a lot of time talking about their death are those who instead believe that it should not be talked about at all. Instead, young people may be faced by a barrier of sentiments such as 'don't talk like that, it will be ok' and 'you just need to be positive, doctors are often wrong'. Young people will frequently refer to the frustration that comes from being 'shutdown' from talking about what they are really worried and thinking about. Particularly pervasive within the common vernacular is the sense that positivity is the answer to the cancer problem. This occurs throughout the time of the young person's cancer, often appearing at the diagnosis, whenever they acknowledge that the treatment is difficult, around periods of relapse and around the end of life. If asked about it, the people speaking about these things can often identify that it may not be helpful, but it provides a buffer from having to address the real concerns that are difficult, uncomfortable and challenging to sit with. Young people are well-versed in sitting with this discomfort, but will generally acknowledge that they make concessions about how they communicate with others about how they feel, and how they are coping to protect them from what they are experiencing. Some, however, can become overwhelmed with the reluctance of those around them to be 'real' about their pending death and sense of urgency, even if they know that the person they are frustrated with knows what is happening. The importance of the therapeutic relationship at this time is paramount, to allow a young person to both speak about death and dying, as well as not talking about it may be the one space that they are 'allowed' to say the most difficult things that cross their minds, or leave them toying with the huge existential challenge that they are faced with.

# Chapter 23

# The end of life

The unfortunate reality of working with young people with cancer is that at times they will not survive their disease. While young people and their doctors may anticipate this from early in the diagnosis, for others a relapse is a jarring surprise and some slip away unexpectedly. Regardless of the situation in which this occurs, this can be a significant challenge for the young people, their families and the healthcare professionals who are around them.

> *Jason is a 19-year-old man diagnosed with advanced stage Hodgkin's disease. He has completed his initial treatment as an outpatient and appeared to have a good response. Treatment had been difficult for him due to anxiety about treatment, and he had a 2-month break before scans showed a relapse. Jason had been very reluctant to have further treatment, and following further cycles of chemotherapy his disease had not responded. He is offered a stem cell transplant, but is aware that the likelihood of the treatment succeeding would be quite low.*

A case such as Jason's can cause significant distress and concern for many health professionals. It is common when this occurs that all those around the young person can become quite panicked and distressed, while the patient can be like the beacon of calm in the storm, watching the chaos around them. Young people have often conceptualised what it might be like should the cancer be unmanageable, or if it returns. In a therapeutic space, there may have been many conversations about their potential death, or risk of such, and the young person may have already been convinced that this would be the outcome long before there has been medical evidence for such. They may have already made decisions about what they want to happen if they were to become more unwell or if the disease returns. The teams caring for the young person are often well aware of the likely trajectory of the disease following failures of treatment, or following multiple relapses, but they will still struggle and have difficulty when they need to make this reality known to a young person and their families. Those around the young person may have some insight to their deterioration (as this rarely happens suddenly, with young people having multiple relapses or complications), but they may have been hopeful that despite what was evident to them, the odds would be overcome.

Regardless of how aware a patient and family are about what is likely to happen, the words surrounding 'you are not going to get better', 'there is nothing more we can do to fix your cancer' or 'you don't have much time now' can trigger a range of potentially unexpected reactions. People who have been clearly articulating the deterioration of their child/self may wail uncontrollably for hours, or those who have been steadfastly declaring their 'fight' against the cancer may acknowledge the news silently. Just like the reactions to diagnosis, relapse and other aspects of the disease, there is no one formulaic approach to help patients and their families cope with this information, and this may need to change from moment to moment, particularly immediately following the change in situation. This time can be very challenging for clinicians as many will oscillate between knowing that they have done everything that they can and that sometimes cancer just behaves this way, and feeling compelled to seek out something to offer the young person.

Human nature does not easily allow us to make sense of young people dying, and for every clinician working in this field there will be certain young patients who 'get under their skin' and challenge the perceptions that we hold to be true about existential meaning and purpose.

Time sometimes helps alleviate the intensity of the emotions patients and their families may have around this news, but changes in their coping are more often related to pragmatic challenges, including deterioration in the patient, caregiving roles, planning for the future (such as needing to make modifications to the home, engaging care services) and ultimately, adjustment to the reality of what they are facing.

As young people approach death, their capacity for engaging in psychological work significantly decreases (as would be expected) and the need for support may shift from the young person to their families and/or the healthcare team looking after them. Young people may feel that they have done all that they need to do psychologically by the time they reach this stage in their disease, or perhaps there are physiological barriers to their ability to engage in discussion and conversation. It is often underestimated how much energy patients require to engage in psychological conversations, particularly when working with confronting concepts such as existential or end-of-life issues. The young person's support network may also be challenged at this time, and interventions may be focused much more on practical support such as helping the carers communicate their needs, nominating a person to communicate what is happening, managing visitors and how to communicate the young person's deterioration to younger siblings or children. Even in this practical intervention, the undertones of the young person's pending death remain and, although at times unspoken, the caregivers identify support around the young person themselves.

'The time that you gave me on that night before he died, it allowed me to work out what I needed in my own head.'
— Mother of a 16-year-old patient

Although a decision will have been made about the palliative status of the young person, there is no guarantee that the young person will deteriorate quickly, and often the opposite is true, with young people often living longer than expected with high disease burdens. This is particularly challenging, especially if the young person has a high symptom load and is incapacitated. There is often an intellectual dichotomy about the ideas around living and dying, and an inherent sense that you cannot be doing both at the same time. Many young patients may live for some time with the knowledge that they are dying, which is a very challenging psychological and existential space to be with periods of complacency creeping in about whether they will really die from the disease. This is more often evident in those who do not have many symptoms, or when the symptoms are well-controlled and they feel relatively well. This is when the challenge of making meaning and purpose in the time that is left can conflict with a negated sense of urgency, paired with overwhelming aware-ness that they are going to die, that may lead to a stagnate inactivity. This inactivity tends to then have the flow-on effect of negative cognition for the patient. Feeling overwhelmed also comes in the form of others' expectations about what it means to be dying, and what they 'should' be doing with that remaining time. For instance, patients can report a sense of needing to have a 'bucket list' but can feel completely over-whelmed by the countless ideas that they could include. It appears that the bucket list is not a particularly helpful tool for young people; instead the therapist can help facilitate activ-ities with the patient around meaning making, and building an idea of what they value. Values-based engagement helps build the foundation for progressing forward with ideas about what they would like to achieve (which may be as simple as spending time with family), rather than a checklist of activities that may be unachievable given the medical reality of their situation.

> 'I should have died months ago. Is it not bad enough that I am dying, that the disease has to torture me as well.'
> — 26-year-old woman

Whenever possible, teams will facilitate young people's engagement in activities that they value at the end of life. For many young people this may involve travel, either for exploration of treatment options overseas, to visit family, return home or simply for the chance to see new places. Although difficult to coordinate, care can often be arranged for young people at the destinations they are travelling to so that if rapid deterioration occurs, or they need medical management, then this is an option. Similarly, for patients who are receiving treatment in tertiary services a long distance away from home, teams will try to coordinate care close to home for the young person, if this is their preference. Deciding where to die is an important decision for a young person and allows them to at least have some sense of control over what is happening for them; however, some patients may defer this decision-making to their parents if they are unwell or unsure about what to do. Even if the tertiary hospital is far from home many may opt to stay and die in the acute ward as the teams, wards and processes are familiar, and young people will often speak of feeling safe with the team that has been with them all through their cancer journey.

> 'I just want to see my dog one more time, then I will come back if I need to.'
> — 23-year-old male

Young people may also opt for a home death, with a hospital as a backup if needed. They will often articulate a sense of feeling more comfortable at home and be reassured by the knowledge that they have their own belongings, familiar surroundings and their peers close by. Furthermore, patients will commonly speak of feeling confronted by the idea of leaving everything for the last time; being at home with all the above aspects can alleviate this for some. Home deaths are well-supported by community palliative care teams who can provide intensive care for patients if needed as they approach death, and provide support and routine for the caregivers or patients. Some of the most important people involved in the decision about whether a young person has a home death may ultimately be those they live with. They are likely to continue living in the house after the young person has died and may feel quite distressed and uneasy about the concept of caring for the dying person at home. This decision can mean a confronting conversation between the young person, their family and the treating team which the therapist may ultimately be involved in or facilitate.

Regardless of the decision of where the young person decides to die, the family and the patient (depending on their medical status) may still choose to have active engagement with the therapist. Of course, it is an individual decision by the therapist about how comfortable or not they may feel around visiting a young person very close to death, or in unfamiliar environments such as a hospice or the young person's home. Visiting families and patients at this time can feel quite intimate and sometimes intrusive so it is very important that if choosing to engage in visits to the patient close to when they die (when they are generally not able to communicate well anymore) the boundaries between clinicians and families are well-established and understood. Following the death of the young patient, the family will likely feel an increased connection with the clinician, which has significant implications around bereavement management. It is also important for the clinician to clarify their reasons for visiting the patient, is it to support the family or is it for the clinician to say goodbye to the young person? Both are very valid reasons to visit, but hey have very disparate outcomes and agendas.

For the therapist, the death of a patient can be a very difficult time, not just due to the emotional gravity of the situation, but the increased logistics/engagement with various teams, family members and health professionals. Following the death of a young person, it is important to give the grief some space, even though it will differ for every young person's death that you see. Ultimately, as clinicians working in this space, the management of grief and bereavement becomes a further thread in the process of engaging with young people living with cancer.

Chapter 24

# Support for the Family After a Young Person Dies

In the oncology setting, the deaths of most young people will be quite expected and families are usually actively involved in the days and weeks leading up to the death. The sense of preparation and acceptance is likely to disappear rapidly, however, following the death of a young person and family members are likely to need support in making sense of their grief and re-engaging in a world outside of the cancer space.

When a young person dies there may be perceived pressure by the family for the treating team to to attend a funeral. Sometimes families may ask specific staff members to attend, and may even request that they play an important role in the service, such as delivery of a eulogy. Healthcare workers are often quite uncertain about the appropriateness of attending funerals, with the decision coming down to an individual's engagement with a particular family. As an individual, it is important that you weigh up what the benefits for the family would be if you were to attend, and ensure that you are not attending for your own grief. If the latter is the case, there are likely to be more-appropriate avenues for such and you are encouraged to seek support or supervision around managing this.

For many families, the cancer hospital and all the processes around it may have been their focus for a considerable time, with the all-consuming nature of it being unrealised until they need to re-engage with what was their former lives. In conjunction with the grief around the loss of their person, there can be loss around the cancer centre and the people themselves as this may have been a significant part of a young person's experience and connections at the end of their lives. There are very few people who understand intimately what their young person went through, and so the connection to the care team may be strong; there is also the sense that the care team are a way of staying connected to the young person.

This connection can present some difficulties for the therapist in terms of ongoing engagement with the family or significant people associated with the young person who has died. Some services have the capacity and are happy to see the families post bereavement for ongoing support, however, in many tertiary services this is not the case. If a family is seeking support there can be difficulties around finding an appropriate person in the community, ending the relationship with the family, and balancing the family's sense of connection and abandonment with the cancer services.

If you were to continue seeing a family member post bereavement, generally they are likely to remain heavily engaged with you for at least a year, with aspects such as first birthdays, Christmas and anniversaries all milestones that will be difficult for them to manage. As with most periods of bereavement, families will generally describe the period between three and six months after the death as the most difficult and may require significant support around this time. For parents, the bereavement process can be particularly complex and may require ongoing support for a long time. If you and your service are unable to provide this level of support, or do not have the expertise to do so, it is paramount that the expectations of what you can provide are given to the family to make sure that they understand what to expect and to not compound the grief further.

A way around this is to offer a set number of sessions after death to allow the person to have a sense of completion with the cancer centre, but this can also be used as a transition time to a new therapist. It is likely that the therapist would have been present for significant milestones in the life of the young person while in treatment, and their family, and the connection and transition needs to be handled very gently. Reassurances to the family that the therapist will give share the medical history and context around the young person's death with the new therapist can help manage the anxiety around having to repeat this to another person. Sometimes there will be a request from the family for the old therapist to be present during the first session with a new therapist to help them feel safe and ensure that all that needs to be covered is addressed. The idea of transitioning away from someone who has known the young person in the context of other loss can be overwhelming, so there may need to be a brief period of transition from talking about the young person and debriefing about their experiences moving towards thinking about their own grief and what it will look like for them to live with it.

After the death, some families will not want to have any contact with the service and will actively avoid any engagement with it as it will be too painful to be back in that space without their child. In this situation, it is much easier to transition someone to an appropriate service in the community if needed. However, for many other families they will hold onto the connection with the treating team and the treating centre for many years after the young person has died. This can be a challenge for team members to manage, however it is important to explore with the families about what it looks like to move away from the centre, and the secondary grief that may come if they disconnect from the cancer centre/hospital.

# Reference List

Cancer Council NSW, 2016. Understanding Chemotherapy; a guide for people with cancer, their families and friends. Available online at http://www. cancer.org.au/content/about_cancer/treatment/ Understanding_Chemotherapy_booklet_August_2016. pdf#_ga=2.260157647.357121741.1500882485-865278777.1500882485

Cancer Council NSW, 2016. Understanding Radiotherapy A guide for people with cancer, their families and friends. Available online at http://www. cancer.org.au/content/about_cancer/treatment/ Understanding%20Radiotherapy_booklet_January%20 2016.pdf#_ga=2.31119485.357121741.1500882485-865278777.1500882485

Leukaemia Foundation Australia, 2017. Stem Cell Transplants. Available online at http://leukaemia.org.au/ treatments/stem-cell-transplants

www.ingramcontent.com/pod-product-compliance
Lightning Source LLC
Chambersburg PA
CBHW050528270326
41926CB00015B/3115